Millennial Kingdom of God on Planet Earth

End-Times Library – Volume 52

Bob Chadwick

MILLENNIAL KINGDOM OF GOD ON PLANET EARTH

•2021•
Second Edition

by Bob Chadwick, LL.M., J.D.
Brigadier General,
United States Marine Corps (Ret.)
copyright © 2021 Bob Chadwick
All rights reserved

Wisdom Press
Box 4888, Carmel, CA 93921
Telephone: (831) 626-3901

E-mail: EndtimesLibrary@outlook.com
Web Site: WisdomPress.org
Available on Amazon.com

ISBN: 9798715845122

No part of this publication may be reproduced, stored in or introduced into a retrieval system, or transmitted, in any form or by any means (electronic, mechanical, photocopying, recording or otherwise), without the prior written permission of the copyright owner.

Dedication

This book is written to and for the faithful Bible-Believing Followers of Jesus who attend our Discovery Class at Carmel Presbyterian Church in Carmel, California, USA (affiliated with the Covenant Order of Evangelical Presbyterians) and to Faithful Followers of Jesus of Nazareth worldwide, as we all prepare for the future, seek a FUTUREFORECAST And ask:

    What's going to happen to me, my family and friends?
    What do we need to know?
    What do we need to do?
    How can we be prepared?
    How can we survive the future?

Watchman's Responsibility

Now, son of man, I am making you a Watchman for the people...
Therefore, listen to what the Lord says and warn them for me.   [cf. Ezekiel 33:7 NLT]

But if the Watchman sees the enemy coming and doesn't sound the alarm to warn the people, he is responsible for their captivity. They will die in their sins, but I will hold the Watchman responsible for their deaths.
    [see Ezekiel 33:6 NLT]

Scripture Citations

Unless otherwise specified, Old Testament citations herein, are from the Christian Standard Bible (CSB) while retaining the American Standard Version's rendering of God's personal name: יהוה into English as **J<u>e</u>hovah***.

New Testament citations are from The World English Bible (WEB) [available at https://www.biblegateway.com/]

---

    * **J<u>e</u>hovah**: The personal, divine name of the LORD God Almighty in the Hebraic text of the Holy Bible is comprised of four Hebrew letters that transliterate into the four English letters **YHVH**. This name of God, used over 6,800 times in the Old Testament, is known as the Tetragrammaton, meaning "the four letters". Proper pronunciation of the Tetragrammaton became obscured when the Jewish people were forbidden to pronounce the name of God to avoid accidently taking his name in vain.

The most recent and most thorough research now reveals that the Hebrew pronunciation is Y<u>e</u>—• ho• **VAH** (English: **J<u>e</u>hovah**) pronounced with three syllables displacing the older prior guess by "experts" of two syllables: Yahweh.

The first letter in the Hebrew name of Jesus (Yeshua) and J<u>e</u>hovah (Yehovah) is the yod. Yod represents the "Y" sound in Hebrew. Many names in the Bible that begin with yod were transliterated in English Bibles with the letter "J" rather than "Y" because in early English the letter "J" was pronounced the way we pronounce "Y" today. And these transliterations have been retained in today's modern English. Hebrew place names as ye-ru-sha-LA-yim, ye-ri-HO, and yar-DEN have become known to us as Jerusalem, Jericho, & Jordan; &Hebrew personal names such as yo-NA, yi-SHAI, yo-sef, ye-SHU-a have become known to us as Jonah, Jesse, Joseph, and Jesus.

    See: Keith Johnson, *His Hallowed Name Revealed Again;*
        Nehemia Gordon *Shattering the Conspiracy of Silence*, p.5;
        Gerard Gertoux, *The Name of God Ye.h.ow.ah;*
        Arnold Fruchtenbaum, *What We Know About God*, 25-26.
    [Listen: http://www.youtube.com/watch?v=wRsbSLU9oFA]

INTRODUCTION

I have many friends and acquaintances who sincerely embrace other religions than Christianity.
It is my sincere desire that they achieve the spiritual fulfillment they seek.

I am a Follower of Jesus of Nazareth, the Messiah (Christ). Jesus declared:
>   I am the way, the truth, and the life.
>   No one comes to the Father (God), except through me.   [John 14:6 World English Bible]

Jesus' declaration is either true or false.

The Word of God also declares about Jesus:
>   No one else can save us. Indeed, we can be saved only by the power of the one named Jesus and not by any other person. [Acts 4:12 God's Word Translation]

I believe both these declarations to be true.
Therefore, I see all other religious systems as less than whole. Yet, the fact that I, as a Follower of Jesus, have this opinion does not mean I look down on the adherents of those other faiths.

To the contrary, I am compelled by deep concern and respect for them to share what I have learned over 91 years of life so that they too can be assured of Eternal Life and entry into the coming Kingdom of God on planet Earth.

Millennial Kingdom of God on Planet Earth

This book is written as a summary guide for Christians to remind everyone what The LORD God Almighty informed the world about the future of planet Earth.

Many learned authors have written in great detail about the vitally important matters summarized herein – for example Dr. Arnold Fruchtenbaum's profound treatise, *The Footsteps of the Messiah*, but unfortunately most people, even avid students of the Christian Bible, have not read his entire 832 page highly recommended volume.

The Compiler realizes that many of the issues discussed herein have a wide range of interpretations within the Christian community and believes we should grant one another grace in interpretations of non-essential beliefs.

CAVEAT

The Compiler gives his personal, non-authoritative understanding of what the Holy Scriptures say about these topics.

It is intended to provide you with an initial starting point for your own individual research and meditation.

Be like the Bereans who "received the WORD with all readiness of the mind, examining the Scriptures daily to see whether these things [being taught] were so." [Acts17:11 WEB]

Use discernment as you read through any materials, testing everything and every author according to the Word of the LORD God Almighty.

These materials represent a composite, for your personal use, of the myriad of resources researched by the Compiler during his 91 years of life.

We all need a little help: a brain to pick and reference sources in addition to original thinking and ideas of our own. In my education I have benefitted and learned from fellowship with and the work of many professionals throughout the world. Their theories, research and ideas have contributed to my thinking and to the underpinnings of this book.
 Any plaudits belong to those professionals while any guffaws or negatives are strictly my own.

Millennial Kingdom of God on Planet Earth

Herein, my goal has been to:
1. **Ensure that timeless truths are kept fresh, alive and continuously communicated;**

2. **Do some of the arduous research for you;**

3. **Reassemble the ideas of many in an easily understood way in one place for your immediate use without your having to expend the time and energy to search out all the background information first;**

   and
4. **Observe the two Golden Rules of Interpretation by**

   a. **not superimposing a preconceived system of interpretation upon the text;**

   and

   b. **not seeking some other sense when the plain sense of Scripture makes common sense while taking every word at its primary, ordinary, usual, literal meaning unless the facts of the immediate context, [studied in the light of related passages and fundamental truths], clearly indicate otherwise.**

On Language

In this book when I write in the third person singular, I use the masculine gender although very often the context refers to both female and male.

As you can see, this work is already long enough without adding further volume by consistently writing "he or she" when using a personal pronoun. And I steadfastly refuse to commit grammatical error by using the plural "they" or a variation thereof with a singular antecedent for the sake of alleged "political correctness".

Therefore, please recognize and understand that I am using a generic "he" and "translate" accordingly.

On Book Recommendations

Please understand that although I have studied and trust each author cited, I am not saying nor am I representing that I necessarily fully agree with everything that the author has written in that particular book.

FAIR USE NOTICE: The information and materials used in this publication may contain copyrighted (©) material the use of which has not always been specifically authorized by the copyright owner. Such material is made available to advance understanding of ecological, political, human rights, economic, democracy, scientific, moral, ethical, and social justice issues, spiritual, religious, etc. It is believed that this constitutes a 'fair use' of any such copyrighted material as provided for in section 107 of the U.S. Copyright Law.

Millennial Kingdom of God on Planet Earth

Other Books by Bob Chadwick

Days of Destiny
  [The Tribulation and Final Seven Years
   of Human Rule on Planet Earth]

Who Removed the Name of God from our Bibles?

Israel's Unique Relationship with the LORD God

Understanding the Day of the LORD

Book of Revelation Reveals the Future of Mankind

  [all available from Amazon.com – search
   under Books - Bob Chadwick on that site]

CONTENTS

1	Has the church of mankind Forgotten Jesus' Gospel of the Kingdom of God?	1
2	What Constitutes a Kingdom?	15
3	What is the Kingdom of God?	17
4	What is Jesus' Gospel of the Kingdom of God?	21
5	The Kingdom Parables	27
6	Where will the Kingdom of God be Established?	31
7	Jesus will be the King	53
8	When will the Kingdom of God be Established?	65
9	Who are the Kingdom's Subjects?	79
10	Duration of the Millennial Kingdom	91
11	Quality of Life in Jesus' Kingdom	103
12	Government of the Kingdom	109

Millennial Kingdom of God on Planet Earth

13	Worship in the Kingdom The Millennial Temple	119
14	Between the Millennium and the Eternal Kingdom	133
15	Eternal Kingdom of God on Earth	141
16	Passport to Enter the Kingdom - Eternal Consequences	149
17	The Final Chorus	157

Appendix I.	Begun in Genesis - Completed in Revelation	163
Appendix II.	End-Times Library	165
Appendix III.	About the Author	173

Chapter One
Has the church of mankind Forgotten Jesus' Gospel of the Kingdom of God?

When Jesus of Nazareth, the Messiah, began his ministry he came preaching the Gospel of the Kingdom of God and Jesus continued his emphasis on that Gospel throughout his ministry.

> <u>Scripture</u>: After John [the Baptist] was put in prison Jesus came into Galilee, preaching the gospel of the kingdom of God.
> [WORD of GOD in Mark 1:14 KJV]

The Gospel of the Kingdom of God is about the literal re-establishment of the Kingdom of God on planet Earth at the Second Coming of Jesus of Nazareth, the Messiah.

And, that Gospel of the Kingdom of God is one of the primary purposes for Jesus' first coming to Earth. As Jesus said specifically:

> I must proclaim the good news about the **Kingdom of God** to the other towns also, because I was sent for this purpose[1]
>
> The Gospel of the Kingdom of God was Jesus' gospel;
>
> the Gospel of the Kingdom of God was Jesus' message;

---
[1] Luke 4:43 [emphasis added].

Millennial Kingdom of God on Planet Earth

> the Gospel of the Kingdom of God was Jesus' purpose;
> the Gospel of the Kingdom of God was the center of Jesus' ministry.

So why do we hear so little about the Kingdom of God—as proclaimed in the Bible—in modern Christianity?

Many adherents to Christianity are not aware of Jesus' central teaching. As a result, it is rarely proclaimed as modern Christianity prefers to dwell on quite different aspects of Jesus' career and teaching.

Think about it. We Christians pray every day:
> "May your kingdom come. May your will be done, **on earth** as it is in heaven."[2]

Yet, in your religious institution you hear over and over again about the Kingdom in Heaven, but only rarely, if ever, about the Kingdom of God on Planet Earth.
Why is that?
Do we really expect or desire what we're praying for?

Have the institutional, bureaucratic religious denominations forgotten, abandoned or just ignored Jesus' central message of the re-establishment of the Kingdom of God on planet Earth at Jesus' Second Coming?

---

[2] Matthew 6:10 International Standard Version [ISV-emphasis added].

Many centuries of religious tradition have convinced people that heaven is their final "home" and their reward.

But, the TRUTHS relating to the Kingdom of God are not determined by the opinions or writings of mankind.

Our starting point must be in the WORD of the LORD God Almighty itself, in context.

And, the biblical record is clear that God's Kingdom will be established on the earth that the LORD God Almighty created, and it will be an everlasting Kingdom on Earth.[3]

From the very beginning and throughout his ministry, Jesus of Nazareth, the Messiah, preached the full Gospel of the Kingdom of God.[4]

The message of Jesus of Nazareth, the Messiah, was not just simply about Himself.
Jesus' words are crystal-clear: the Kingdom of God is to be the central focus and emphasis in the lives of his Faithful Followers:

>But, seek **first** the Kingdom of God and his

---

[3] See Psalm 2:6-8; 47:1-9; Jeremiah 23:5; Ezekiel 37:21-28; Daniel 2:44-45; 7:17-18, 27; Micah 4:1-5; Zechariah 9:9-10; 14:9, 16-17; Revelation 2:26-27 [ISV]
[4] Luke 8;1, 16:16; Matthew 9:35

Millennial Kingdom of God on Planet Earth

> righteousness, and all these things will be provided for you.[5]

Then Jesus went to all the towns and villages, teaching in their synagogues, preaching the good news *[gospel]* of the Kingdom.[6]

> He *[Jesus]* told them, 'I have to proclaim the good news about the kingdom of God in other cities, because I was sent to do that' …[7]

> Now after John had been arrested, Jesus went to Galilee and proclaimed the gospel about the kingdom of God. He said, "The time is now! The kingdom of God is near! Repent, and keep believing the gospel!"[8]

Then he [Jesus] went throughout Galilee, teaching in their synagogues, proclaiming the gospel of the kingdom, and healing every disease and every illness among the people.[9]

After this, Jesus traveled from one city and village to another, preaching and spreading the good news *[gospel]* about God's kingdom. The Twelve were with

---

[5] Matthew 6:33 [emphasis added]
[6] Matthew 9:35
[7] Luke 4:43 [ISV]
[8] Mark 1:14-15 [ISV]
[9] Matthew 4:23 [ISV]

him.[10]

> The Law and the Prophets were fulfilled with John *[the Baptist]*. Since then, the good news about the kingdom of God is being proclaimed, and everybody enters it enthusiastically.[11]
>
> And this Gospel of the Kingdom will be proclaimed throughout the inhabited world as a testimony to all nations, and **then the end will come.**"[12]

The inspired Word of God makes it abundantly plain: the "good news" that Jesus Christ brought was about the Kingdom of God!

The "Gospel of Jesus Christ" is simply the message of good news *that Jesus preached.* It is not primarily a message about the events in His life and of His becoming the Savior of the world—although it most certainly does include all that.

But if the events of His life are not seen in the context of what He *said* about the Kingdom of God, the resulting "faith" could be incomplete.

---

[10] Luke 8:1 [ISV]
[11] Luke 16:16-17 [ISV]
[12] Matthew 24:14 [emphasis added] [ISV]

Millennial Kingdom of God on Planet Earth

The announcement of "good news"—the very best news that could be heard today—which the Father gave through Jesus Christ, was about His Kingdom being established on earth.

And, upon further reflection, we find that the Biblical story of the Kingdom of God on planet Earth begins well before the time period of Jesus' first coming.

THE KINGDOM OF GOD IN GENESIS

The theme of a future, earthly Kingdom of God on Planet Earth begins in the first book of the Holy Bible: Genesis.[13]

In the Garden of Eden, the LORD God Almighty placed Adam and Eve in a position of authority over God's creation.[14] Adam and Eve were given authority over the physical realm (fish, birds, living things that move on the earth).

Humanity's first couple was to govern God's creation on God's behalf, serving as Theocratic Administrators. God ruled the world indirectly through the firstAdam.[15]

But, Adam and Eve were influenced by Satan to rebel

---

[13] Dr. Andy Woods, *The Coming Kingdom*, Part I., p.5
[14] Genesis 126-28 [ISV]
[15] Dr. Andy Woods, *The Coming Kingdom*, Part I., p.3

against God and they were expelled from the Garden.[16]

Satan's success in inciting this rebellion effectively removed the office of Theocratic Administrator from the earth, as Satan became the ruler of the world.[17]

But, the WORD of God assures us that in the future, through the Messianic Millennial Kingdom of Jesus Christ on Planet Earth, God the Father will restore what was lost in Eden.[18]

After Jesus was resurrected he founded his Christian Church at Pentecost – a called out group of Faithful Followers – to carry out the work, he, Jesus was doing while on Earth and the Faithful Group was to go into the entire world to preach the same message he, Jesus, preached while on Earth.[19]

And, the WORD of the LORD God Almighty in the book of Acts establishes that the early Faithful Christian Church followed Jesus' command and preached the Gospel of the Kingdom of God to the world[20] as Faithful Followers in that early Church focused on the coming Kingdom of God.[21]

---

[16] Genesis 3:23 [ISV]
[17] Luke 4:5-8; John 12:31; 14:30; 16:11; 2 Corinthians 4:4; Ephesians 2:2
[18] Revelation 20:4-6
[19] Matthew 24:14, 28:19-20; Mark 16:15; Acts 1:3-8
[20] Acts 8:12, 14:22, 19:8, 20:25, 28:31, 33
[21] Colossians 4:11; 2nd Thessalonians 1:5

Millennial Kingdom of God on Planet Earth

The Apostles recognized with crystal clarity that, when Jesus spoke of the Kingdom of God, he spoke in terms of a real government—a structured, organized entity with the very authority of God behind it.

Certain rulers who heard Christ's message recognized the political implications and viewed his words as a threat to their own power. This became a factor in Christ's eventual crucifixion.[22]

To Jesus and his Apostles, the term Kingdom of God meant a government that would be established on earth. They anticipated that its arrival would amount to nothing less than a sweeping, overwhelming change in the world order.

This view was widely held in the Early Church and was expounded by the Church fathers Papias, Irenaeus, and Tertullian.[23]

But, as time went on the intense focus on the coming earthly Kingdom of God began to wane, became minimized and then abandoned after the end of the New Testament era.

---

[22] Luke 23:2; John 19:12
[23] *Collier's Encyclopedia,* 1993, *Millennium.*

ROMAN EMPEROR CONSTANTINE & CHRISTIANITY

One of the key precipitative factors in this decline of focus on the coming Kingdom of God was the Roman Emperor Constantine's decision to cease the persecution of Christians in the Roman Empire.

In 313 A.D. Constantine and Licinius issued the Edict of Milan decriminalizing Christian worship.
Although Nicene Christianity did not become the state church of the Roman Empire until Emperor Theodosius I. made it the Empire's sole authorized religion with the Edict of Thessalonica in 380 AD, Constantine became a great patron of the Church and set a precedent for the position of the Christian emperor.

Constantine is revered as a saint by the Eastern Orthodox Church for his example as a "Christian monarch."

Historians remain uncertain about Constantine's reasons for favoring Christianity, and theologians and historians have often argued about which form of early Christianity he subscribed to. Some scholars question the extent to which he should be considered a Christian emperor although he allegedly was baptized shortly before his death in 337 A.D.

Millennial Kingdom of God on Planet Earth

An early political-ecclesiastical alliance was forged between Eusebius Pamphilius[24] and the Emperor Constantine. Constantine, regarding himself as God's representative in his role as emperor, gathered all the bishops together on the day of the 30th anniversary of his reign, an event which he saw as the foreshadowing of the future Messianic banquet.

The results of that meeting, in Eusebius' mind, made it unnecessary to distinguish any longer between the church and the Empire, for they appeared to merge into one already fulfilled kingdom of God on earth at that present time.
    Such a move abandoned Jesus' and the early Church's focus on a future Kingdom of God on Earth and also removed the role and the significance of the Jewish people in any future kingdom considerations as well.

By this time the church had become overwhelmingly Gentile reinforcing the concept that the Jews have no role in future events.

---

[24] Eusebius of Caesarea, *also known as Eusebius Pamphili* (260-340 A.D. is often called the father of church history. He was probably born in Caesarea, Palestine and had Pamphilius as his teacher. His works are of a theological and apologetic nature.

He became one of the earliest and most influential bishops of the Christian Church. According to survival records of the Church Council of Nicaea, he occupied the first seat on the right of the Emperor and delivered the inaugural address on the Emperor's behalf.

[per Philip Schaff, *Nicene and Post-Nicene Fathers, vol 1*]

Historian Justo Gonzalez writes:

> Since the time of Constantine, and due in part to the work of Eusebius and of many others of similar theological orientation, there was a tendency to set aside or to postpone the hope of the early church, that its Lord would return in the clouds to establish a Kingdom of peace and justice. ...
>
> Eusebius, although more articulate than most, was simply expressing the common feeling among Christians, for whom the advent of Constantine and of the peace he brought about was the final triumph of Christianity over its enemies".[25]

This idea was also promoted by the theologian Augustine of Hippo[26] in his highly influential book *The City of God,* where Augustine said: "Therefore the Church even now is the kingdom of Christ, and the kingdom of heaven" (Book XX, Chapter 9). And Augustine advanced the theory that the millennium had actually begun with Christ's nativity.[27] And, the church then officially adopted Augustine's view that the biblical descriptions of the millennium were allegorical and not an actual 1,000 years as the Biblical text explicitly says six times in the first seven verses of Chapter 20 of the Book of Revelation.[28]

---

[25] *The Story of Christianity*, Vol. 1, pp. 134-135
[26] A.D. 354-430
[27] *New Catholic Encyclopedia,* 1967, *Millenarianism.*
[28] *Encyclopedia Americana,* 1998, *Millennium.*

Millennial Kingdom of God on Planet Earth

And Augustine's beliefs continue as prominent beliefs (in different forms) in mainstream Christianity today as many theologians lose faith in the Bible's plain teaching that at his Second Coming Jesus of Nazareth, the Messiah will reign from Jerusalem over the earth in a literal Messianic Millennial Kingdom.

After the true biblical teaching of the Kingdom of God was removed, the gospel message was changed from the full message about the future Kingdom to a message primarily about the means to gain entry to the Kingdom and the contention that the institutional church had already brought the Kingdom into being.[29]

Further, we now know that in actual fact, Emperor Constantine believed in Mithraism: the elaborate pagan worship of the Sun-god that dominated the Roman Empire during the time of Christ. Mithraism was an evolvement of the Babylonian Mystery Religion founded by Nimrod at Babel. When God scattered the people of Babel over the earth, the mystery cults of the Sun-God and the Mother-Goddess permeated all the religions of the world.[30]

"As seen in Constantine's originated piety, his supreme deity would have been associated with the

---

[29] See p. 28 and Chapter 10 hereof for further discussion of this contention.
[30] Carmen F. Johnson, *Commentary on Constantine's Sword*, p. 18 retrieved at http://www.arielministries.net/ariel0621.html

sun. Pagans would have recognized, with reason, their own solar cult in such "Christian" practices as orienting Churches to the east: worshiping on "Sunday": celebrating the resurrection of Ishtar on the Vernal Equinox (Easter): and the birth of the Sun-god at the Winter Solstice......there was a lack of religious clarity in Constantine's own mind."[31]

History confirms that Constantine merely co-mingled the worship of the Sun-god with his created mutation of "Christianity". In this way, he single-handedly saved a weakened and crumbling Roman Empire. By marrying the political and religious life of all Romans into a heady cocktail of paganism and Christianity,[32] he gained absolute control of the Empire.

Even so, Constantine was called the "new Moses" by his new "church".

---

[31] Edward Flannery, *Constantine's Sword*, p. 183

[32] Consider our calendar weekdays named for visible celestial bodies associated with pagan deities: Sunday named in honor of the Sun god; Monday named in honor of the Moon god; Saturday-planet Saturn named in honor of the Roman god Saturn.
And calendar months: January (Januarius) in honor of the Roman god Janus; March (Martius) in honor of the Roman god Mars, June (Junius) in honor of the Roman goddess Juno; July(Julius) in honor of the Roman emperor Julius Caesar; and August (Augustus) in honor of the Roman emperor Augustus Caesar. [see Hutton Webster, *Rest Days*, 220-221].

AN INVITATION

I invite you to join with me and enter the fascinating and spiritually enriching world of Biblical knowledge compiled herein for you.

Grant me the honor of being your guide to an overview of the LORD God Almighty's master plan for our future.[33]

And, as we proceed remember to act as a good Berean[34] by checking and testing everything I have to say against Scripture, history and reality.

---

[33] Adapted from Dr. David Reagan, *The Master Plan*, p. 17.
[34] Acts 17:10-11

Chapter Two
What Constitutes a Kingdom?

But what is a kingdom?

A Kingdom is essentially a nation with all its citizens, land, and laws, ruled by a royal authority, a monarch: king or queen or an authorized administrator.

A kingdom has five basic elements:
1. a royal authority – a King or Queen or authorized administrator;
2. territory - with specific location and definite boundary lines;
3. subjects or citizens within that territorial jurisdiction;
4. laws and a form of government through which the will of the ruler is exercised; and
5. a duration.

Accordingly, a kingdom must have a royal authority who rules by law over a number of subjects who live within a certain territory.

If we ignore any one of these essential elements—if we ignore the message that Jesus Christ brought from the Father—we will have a distorted faith.[35]

---

[35] *What Did Jesus Preach*, retrieved at http://www.truegospel.org/index.cfm/fuseaction/basics.tour/ID/2/What-Did-Jesus-Preach.htm

Millennial Kingdom of God on Planet Earth

Chapter Three
What is the Kingdom of God?

THE KINGDOM OF GOD
The Kingdom of God is the specific territory ruled by the eternal, sovereign LORD God Almighty wherein evil is fully overcome and God's Faithful Followers dwell knowing only happiness, peace and joy.[36]

The Kingdom of God has the five basic elements of any kingdom:
    (1) royal authority,
    (2) territory,
    (3) citizens/subjects,
    (4) laws and government; and
    (5) duration
with a member of the Holy Trinity: God the Father, God the Son or the Holy Spirit as the royal authority.

And, the Kingdom of God adds a sixth element: Visible Presence of Shekinah Glory.
Whenever the Kingdom of God is present on planet Earth, the visible Shekinah Glory is also present.

The Kingdom of God has four manifestations:
    1. The Universal Kingdom of God;

---

[36] Ronald Youngblood, editor, *Nelson's New Illustrated Bible Dictionary*, p.729

2. Initial Presence of the Kingdom of God on planet Earth in Eden;
3. Future 1,000 Year Messianic Millennial Kingdom of God, the Son, on Earth; and
4. Future Eternal State- permanent Presence of the Kingdom of God on planet Earth.

THE UNIVERSAL KINGDOM OF GOD

The Universal Kingdom of God is the eternal sovereign, providential rule of the LORD God Almighty over his creation. No matter where things exist in God's creation everything is within his sovereign will and control.[37]

INITIAL PRESENCE OF KINGDOM OF GOD ON PLANET EARTH IN EDEN

The theme of an earthly Kingdom of God begins in the Bible's very first chapter.
The history of the Kingdom of God on planet Earth begins in the Garden of Eden.

In the Garden of Eden God placed the First Adam and Eve in a position of authority, as God's

---

[37] 1st Chronicles 29:11-12; Psalm 10:16; Psalm 29:10, Psalm 90:1-6; Psalm 93:1-5; Psalm 103:19-22; Psalm 145:1-21; Psalm 148:1-14; Jeremiah 10:10; Lamentations 5:19; Daniel 4: 17, 25, 32; Daniel 6:26; Dr. Arnold Fruchtenbaum, *Footsteps of the Messiah*, p. 662.

Administrators, over God's creation.[38]

But, Satan succeeded in inciting Adam's rebellion and effectively removed the office of God's [Theocratic] Administrator from the earth, as Satan became the temporary ruler of the world.[39]

But, Satan's rule is only temporary.

One day God the Father will restore what was lost in Eden. And, he will again rule the world indirectly through an intermediary.

This intermediary will not be the original Adam but rather the Last Adam or the unique God-man Jesus Christ who is the second member of the Trinity.

And, just as God, the Father originally intended to indirectly govern the physical world through the first Adam, God, the Father, will during the Millennium govern the world through the Last Adam or God, the Son.[40]

Future Messianic Millennial Kingdom of God, the Son, on planet Earth

The future Messianic Millennial Kingdom is

---

[38] Genesis 1:26-28
[39] Luke 4:5-8; John 12:31, 14:30, 16:11; 2nd Corinthians 4:4; Ephesians 2:2
[40] Revelation 20:1-7; 1st Corinthians 15:20-28, 45-8

<u>Millennial Kingdom of God on Planet Earth</u>

considered in Chapters 6-14 hereof.

THE FUTURE ETERNAL STATE- PERMANENT PRESENCE OF THE KINGDOM OF GOD ON PLANET EARTH

After God the Son's thousand-year Messianic Millennial Kingdom and the reformation of the Earth[41] the New Jerusalem will descend to Earth and God, the Father will join God, the Son to live in the New Jerusalem on Planet Earth for eternity.[42]

The Eternal State is discussed in Chapter 15 hereof.

---

[41] 2nd Peter 3:10
[42] Revelation 21:1-4, 22; Revelation 22:3-4

Chapter Four
What is Jesus' Gospel of the Kingdom of God?

The phrase Gospel of the Kingdom and references to "the Kingdom of God" and "the Kingdom of Heaven" are used repeatedly in connection with the Lord Jesus and His work on earth.

The word "Gospel" means "good news," and the term translated "kingdom" is the Greek word *basileia*, which means "the realm in which a sovereign king rules."

THE KINGDOM OF GOD AND THE KINGDOM OF HEAVEN

Although some teachers believe that the phrases Kingdom of God and Kingdom of Heaven are referring to different things, it is clear that both phrases refer to and mean the same thing.

The phrase "Kingdom of God" occurs 63 times in nine different New Testament books, while "Kingdom of Heaven" occurs only 31 times, and only in the Gospel of Matthew.

The reason for Matthew's exclusive use of the phrase is the Jewish nature of his Gospel. Matthew uses the term "Kingdom of Heaven" to avoid offending the sensibilities of his target audience: the Jewish people.

Among the Jewish people there was a special sensitivity about writing out the word "God".
Even today, Orthodox Jews will not write out the word "god" but instead will write "G – d".

This tendency in Judaism is to show respect for the term by using a substitute. Often, rather than using the word "God", they will use the term "Heaven". This is common in rabbinical literature – both the *Mishnah* and the *Gemara* which make up the *Talmud* – where the term "Kingdom of Heaven" is used to mean "Kingdom of God".
The terms are used interchangeably.[43]

Also, in the Biblical text, Christ uses "kingdom of heaven" and "kingdom of God" interchangeably. In speaking to the rich young ruler, said to his disciples, "I assure you, it will be hard for a rich person to enter the kingdom of heaven" (Matthew 19:23). In the very next verse, Christ proclaims, "Again I tell you, it is easier for a camel to go through the eye of a needle than for a rich person to enter the kingdom of God" (verse 24). Jesus makes no distinction between the two terms but seems to consider them synonymous.

---

[43] Dr. Arnold Fruchtenbaum, Footsteps of the Messiah, p.661.

Mark and Luke used "kingdom of God" where Matthew used "kingdom of heaven" frequently in parallel accounts of the same parable. Compare Matthew 11:11-12 with Luke 7:28; Matthew 13:11 with Mark 4:11 and Luke 8:10; Matthew 13:24 with Mark 4:26; Matthew 13:31 with Mark 4:30 and Luke 13:18; Matthew 13:33 with Luke 13:20; Matthew 18:3 with Mark 10:14 and Luke 18:16; and Matthew 22:2 with Luke 13:29.

In each instance, Matthew used the phrase "kingdom of heaven" while Mark and/or Luke used "kingdom of God." Clearly, the two phrases refer to the same thing.

GOSPEL OF THE KINGDOM OF GOD

The Gospel of the Kingdom of God is the good-news message that we Faithful Followers of Jesus of Nazareth, the Messiah:

- have a King, Jesus, God the son;[44]
- our King has adopted us, his Faithful Followers into his royal family;[45]
- our King will come again to planet Earth [the Second Coming];[46]
- our King will establish an actual, literal, physical Messianic Kingdom on Earth;[47]

---

[44] Daniel 7:13-14; Zechariah 14:1, 9; Jeremiah 23:5; Isaiah 9:6-7
[45] Ephesians 1:4,5,7,8; Ephesians 2:19; 1st Peter 2:9; Revelation 1:5-6
[46] Revelation 19:11-16
[47] Zechariah 14:1, 9; Daniel 7:13-14

> our King will rule from Jerusalem for 1,000 years from the Throne established by King David of Israel;[48]
> our King will establish justice and righteousness making all things right;[49]
> at the end of his 1,000-year reign, our King will merge his Messianic Millennial Kingdom into the Universal Kingdom of God, the Father in the New Jerusalem;[50]
>> and,
> our King will reign forever on Earth with God, the Father and God, the Holy Spirit.[51]

When Jesus speaks about the kingdom of God coming near,[52] he is referring to something truly revolutionary.

He means that with his own coming to earth, God's saving rule and reign has come near in a way that's never happened before in all of human history.

He means that God's promises to establish his kingdom are beginning to be fulfilled, and that God will one day usher in a new creation, which has even now been inaugurated through Jesus' resurrection.[53]

---

[48] Isaiah 9:6-7; Revelation 20:2-6; see Jeremiah 23:5
[49] Jeremiah 23:5; see also Jeremiah 33:14-16
[50] 1st Corinthians 15:24-28; Revelation chapters 21-22
[51] Daniel 2:44; Revelation chapter 21:21-27
[52] Mark 1:15
[53] Colossians 1:18; 2nd Corinthians 5:17

This new creation will be a place of perfect righteousness and peace, a place in which all wrongs will be made right.[54]

The gospel of the kingdom is the good-news message of repentance, redemption, and restoration offered by God to all who will receive Christ. Those who accept this offer become part of His eternal kingdom.[55]

Although grace makes this offer available to anyone who will receive it, Jesus warned that it would be very difficult to enter His Kingdom and few would do so.[56]

Our Redeemer has come, but it is difficult to enter God's kingdom, not because God requires impossible standards for us, but because we do not want to repent and change. We tend to love the darkness more than the Light.[57]

Many would rather cling to their old sinful identities than allow Jesus to create them anew.[58]

Those who choose to remain in their unrighteousness cannot become a part of the Kingdom of God.[59]

---

[54] Revelation 21:1-5; https://www.9marks.org/answer/what-gospel-kingdom/
[55] John 1:12
[56] Matthew 7:14
[57] John 3:19
[58] 2nd Corinthians 5:17
[59] 1st Corinthians 6:9-10; Galatians 5:19-21.

Millennial Kingdom of God on Planet Earth

Jesus said, "My kingdom is not of this world".[60]
Those who accept the Gospel of the Kingdom become citizens of the Kingdom and are freed from bondage to this world.[61] So, although we must live here until God calls us home, we are not to live for ourselves or according to this world's value system. Those who have been bought by the blood of Jesus have been given the right to live according to God's value system.

Citizens of the Kingdom of God live here on assignment from our Father the King.
Living with a kingdom mindset empowers us to make wiser decisions as we invest our lives in furthering the gospel of the kingdom.

Second Corinthians 5:20 refers to God's children as "Ambassadors" for our heavenly Father. Just as an earthly foreign ambassador retains his national identity when representing his country in another, the spiritual ambassadors of God's Kingdom owe their allegiance to God even as they reside in this world. We must follow our heavenly Father's code of conduct while we are sojourners on earth. We need not necessarily conform to this world's habits, values, and lifestyle, because this is not our home.[62]

---

[60] John 18:36
[61] Galatians 4:3-9
[62] Romans 12:1–2; 1st John 2:15–17

Chapter Five
The Kingdom Parables

The eight Kingdom parables of Matthew chapter 13 are understood harmoniously; they reveal a complete picture of the spiritual conditions that will prevail in the world during this current interim period when the Kingdom of God is not physically and visibly present on planet Earth.[63]

First, the Parable of the Sower teaches that the gospel will be preached throughout the course of this interim age with varying responses based upon how the heart has been prepared. Responders to the truth will be given additional revelation.[64]

Second, the Parable of the Wheat and The Weeds teaches that it will be difficult to distinguish between the saved and unsaved within professing Christendom throughout this current age. The separation between believer and unbeliever will not be made until the "harvest" which is the Second Advent [Jesus' return to Planet Earth].[65]

---

[63] Adapted from Dr. Andy Woods, *The Coming Kingdom* Part 7, retrieved at http://www.pre-trib.org/articles/view/the-coming-kingdom-7,
[64] Matthew 13:1-9, 18-23
[65] Matthew 13: 24-30, 36-43

Millennial Kingdom of God on Planet Earth

Third, the Parable of the Mustard Seed teaches that Christendom will experience great numerical and geographical expansion from a small beginning.[66]

Fourth, because leaven in Scripture typically represents something pernicious or evil,[67] the Parable of the Leaven working its way through the meal teaches that professing Christendom will experience increasing moral and doctrinal corruption as the age progresses.[68] This parable predicts increasing apostasy throughout the present church age and is consistent with the doctrine of Scripture concerning the evil character of the end of the church age and the Tribulation.[69]

Understanding this increasing apostasy represents a worldview that is diametrically opposed to "Kingdom Now" theology which is the idea that the church will gradually Christianize the world and usher in long-term cultural progress.[70]

Fifth, because Scripture refers to Israel as God's special treasure,[71] the Parable of the Earthen Treasure teaches that Jesus came to redeem Israel.

---

[66] Matthew 13:31-32
[67] Exodus 12; Leviticus 2:11, 6:17, 10:12; Matthew 16:6, 12; Mark 8:15; Luke 12:1; 1st Corinthians 5:6-8; Galatians 5:9
[68] Matthew 13:33
[69] 1st Timothy 4; 2nd Timothy 3; Jude; 2nd Peter 3; Revelation 6–19
[70] Dr. Andy Woods, *The Coming Kingdom* Part 7, retrieved at http://www.pre-trib.org/articles/view/the- coming-kingdom-7,
[71] Exodus 19:5

However, Israel will remain in unbelief throughout the course of the current church age and will not be converted until the church age's conclusion.[72]

Sixth, the Parable of the Hidden Treasure & Pearl of Great Price refers to Christ's death that redeems members of the church throughout this age allowing the Lord to gain a treasure from among the Gentiles.[73]

Seventh, the Parable of the Fishing Net teaches the coexistence of the righteous and the wicked throughout the current age only to be separated by Christ during the Judgment of the Sheep and the Goats at the Messiah's Second Coming.[74]

Eighth, the Parable of the Householder teaches that these current aspects of the Kingdom must be considered alongside Old Testament Kingdom truth if one is to understand the totality of God's kingdom agenda.[75]

---

[72] Matthew 13:44
[73] Matthew 13:45-46
[74] Matthew 13:47-50; Matthew 25:31-46
[75] Matthew 13:51-52

Millennial Kingdom of God on Planet Earth

Chapter Six
Where will the Kingdom of God be Located?

Many people assume that the Millennial Kingdom of God is located in heaven, but this Compiler believes that the Bible clearly teaches that when Jesus Christ returns, the Kingdom of God will be established on Planet Earth![76]

Remember Isaiah's original Promise:
> For a child will be born for us, a son will be given to us,
> and the government will be on His shoulders.
> He will be named Wonderful Counselor,
> Mighty God, Eternal Father, Prince of Peace.
>
> The dominion will be vast, and its prosperity will never end.
> He will reign on the throne of David and over his kingdom, to establish and sustain it with justice and righteousness from now on and forever.

---

[76] For a discussion of the basic viewpoints on the Biblical texts concerning the Millennium and when the Millennium occurs in relation to the timing of the Second Coming of Jesus of Nazareth, the Messiah, to planet Earth see Chapter 24 of Bob Chadwick, *Days of Destiny- the Tribulation and Final Seven Years of Human Rule on Planet Earth. [available at Amazon.com]*.

Millennial Kingdom of God on Planet Earth

The zeal of the Lord of Hosts will accomplish this.   **[WORD of GOD in Isaiah 9:6-7]**[77]

Similarly, Jeremiah writes,
> **"The days are coming"—this is the Lord's declaration—"when I will raise up a Righteous Branch of David.**
> **He will reign wisely as king and administer justice and righteousness in the land.**
> **In His days Judah will be saved, and Israel will dwell securely.**
> **This is what He will be named: J<u>e</u>hovah Our Righteousness.**
>   **[WORD of GOD in Jeremiah 23:5-6]**

Remember the angel Gabriel's promise to the Virgin Mary in Nazareth:
> **Do not be afraid, Mary, for you have found favor with God.**
> **Now listen: You will conceive and give birth to a son, and you will call His name Jesus.**
>
> **He will be great and will be called the Son of the Most High, and the Lord God will give Him the throne of His father David.**
> **He will reign over the house of Jacob forever, and His kingdom will have no end.**
>   **[WORD of GOD in Luke 1:30-33]**

---

[77] Emphasis added in all cited scriptures.

Remember Jesus' promise to his Disciples:
> I assure you: In the Messianic Age, when the Son of Man sits on His glorious throne, you who have followed Me will also sit on 12 thrones, judging the 12 tribes of Israel.
> [WORD of GOD in Matthew 19:28]

Are we Christians actually sincere when we pray each and every day:
> Your kingdom come. Your will be done **On earth** as it is in heaven.
> [WORD of GOD in Matthew 6:10]

As the Elders sang to Jesus as Jesus was about to open the sealed scroll:
> You are worthy to take the scroll, And to open its seals;
> For You were slain, And have redeemed us to God by Your blood
> Out of every tribe and tongue and people and nation,
> And have made us kings and priests to our God;
> And we shall reign **on the earth**.
> [WORD of GOD-Revelation 5:9-10 NKJV, emphasis added]

And, Jesus' reign will not be just of Israel and Judah, but will also extend over the entire earthly world:

Millennial Kingdom of God on Planet Earth

>The seventh angel blew his trumpet: And there were loud voices of heaven, saying, 'The kingdoms of **this world** have become *the kingdoms* of our Lord and of His Messiah, and He shall reign forever and ever!'
>>[WORD of GOD in Revelation 11:15]

And, as Jesus returns from Heaven to Earth:
>the armies [from] heaven followed Him on white horses wearing pure white linen. A sharp sword came from His mouth, so that He might strike the nations with it. He will shepherd them with an iron scepter. He will also trample the winepress of the fierce anger of God, the Almighty. And He has a name written on His robe and on His thigh::
>>KING OF KINGS AND LORD OF LORDS.
>>>[WORD of GOD in Revelation 19:14-16]

>On that day His feet will stand on the Mount of Olives, which faces Jerusalem on the east. The Mount of Olives shall be split in half from east to west, forming a huge valley, so that half the mountain shall move to the north and half to the south.
>>[WORD of GOD in Zechariah 14:4]

And he who overcomes, and keeps My works
until the end, to him I will give power over the
nations—
He shall rule them with a rod of iron;
They shall be dashed to pieces like the
potter's vessel;
    [WORD of GOD in Revelation 2:26-27 NKJV]

In the last days the mountain of the LORD's
house
Shall be established at the top of the mountains,
And will be raised above the hills;
All nations will stream to it.
        [WORD of GOD in Isaiah 2:2]

I have consecrated My King on **Zion**, My holy
mountain.
I will declare the Lord's decree:
He [the LORD] said to Me, You *are* My Son,
Today I have become your Father.
Ask of Me, and I will make the nations Your
inheritance,
And the **ends of the earth** Your possession.
        [WORD of GOD in Psalms 2:6-8]

The kingdom, dominion, and greatness of the
kingdoms under all of heaven,
will be given to the people, the holy ones of the
Most High.

Millennial Kingdom of God on Planet Earth

His kingdom will be an everlasting kingdom, and all rulers will serve and obey Him.
[WORD of GOD in Daniel 7:27]
On that day Jehovah will become King over all the earth. Jehovah alone, and His name alone. [WORD of GOD in Zechariah 14:9]

Then I saw thrones, and people seated on them who were given authority to judge. I also saw the people who had been beheaded because of their testimony about Jesus and because of God's word, who had not worshiped the beast or his image, and who had not accepted the mark on their foreheads or their hands.

They came to life and reigned with the Messiah for 1,000 years. The rest of the dead did not come to life until the 1,000 years were completed. This is the first resurrection. Blessed and holy is the one who shares in the first resurrection! The second death has no power over them, but they will be priests of God and of the Messiah, and they will reign with Him for 1,000 years. [WORD of GOD in Revelation 20:4-6]

Then I saw a new heaven and a new earth, for the first heaven and the first earth had passed away, and the sea no longer existed. I also saw the Holy City, new Jerusalem, coming down

out of heaven from God, prepared like a bride adorned for her husband.

Then I heard a loud voice from the throne: Look! **God's dwelling is with humanity**, and He will live with them. They will be His people, and God Himself will be with them and be their God.
        [WORD of GOD in Revelation 21:1-3]

Isaiah described that Millennial Kingdom:
    The wolf also shall dwell with the lamb,
    The leopard shall lie down with the young goat,
    The calf and the young lion and the fatling together;
    And a little child shall lead them.
    The cow and the bear shall graze;
    Their young ones shall lie down together;
    And the lion shall eat straw like the ox.
    The nursing child shall play by the cobra's hole,
    And the weaned child shall put his hand in the viper's den.
    They shall not hurt nor destroy in all My holy mountain,
    For the earth shall be full of the knowledge of the LORD
    As the waters cover the sea.
        [WORD of GOD in Isaiah 11:6-9] NKJV]

Millennial Kingdom of God on Planet Earth

It shall come to pass in that day
***That* the Lord shall set His hand again the second time**
To recover the remnant of His people who are left *[survive]*,
From Assyria and Egypt, From Pathros and Cush *[Ethiopia]*,
From Elam *[in Iran]* and Shinar *[Babylonia]*,
From Hamath *[region near Aleppo, Syria]* and the islands of the sea.
He will set up a banner for the nations, and will assemble the outcasts of Israel,
And gather together the dispersed of Judah from the four corners of the earth.
Also the envy of Ephraim shall depart, and the adversaries of Judah shall be cut off; Ephraim shall not envy Judah, and Judah shall not harass Ephraim.
                    [WORD of GOD in Isaiah 11:11-13]

On that day the Lord will thresh grain from the Euphrates River
as far as the Wadi of Egypt, and you Israelites will be gathered one by one.
On that day a great trumpet will be blown, and those lost in the land of Assyria will come, as well as those dispersed in the land of Egypt; and they will worship the Lord at Jerusalem on the holy mountain.
                    [WORD of GOD in Isaiah 27:12

The prophet Micah foretold that the Messiah coming out of Bethlehem, would be the One to be ruler in Israel and his greatness will extend to the **ends of the earth.** [WORD of GOD in Micah 5:2-4]

> I will declare the Lord's decree: He said to Me, "You are My Son; today I have become Your Father.
> Ask of Me, and I will make the nations Your inheritance and the ends of the earth Your possession.
> [WORD of GOD in Psalm 2:7-8]

> When that Kingdom is established,
> All the ends of the earth will remember and turn to the Lord.
>   All the families of the nations will bow down before You, for kingship belongs to the Lord; He rules over the nations.
>   All who prosper on earth will eat and bow down; all those who go down to the dust will kneel before Him— …
> Their descendants will serve Him; the next generation will be told about the Lord.
> [WORD of GOD in Psalm 22:27-30]

While it is a given that God is sovereign over the earth, it is also painfully obvious from looking around us today that this prophecy of the world turning to

Millennial Kingdom of God on Planet Earth

Him has yet to be fulfilled:
> **Then all the survivors from the nations that came against Jerusalem will go up year after year to worship the King, the Lord of Hosts, and to celebrate the Festival of Booths.** *[Tabernacles]*
> [WORD of GOD in Zechariah 14:16]

God made promises and recorded prophecies about the coming King as far back as Abraham's time. He made the first promise, though not detailed, to the patriarch when he was 99 years old, just after God made a covenant with him and changed his name saying. "I will make you extremely fruitful and will make nations and *kings come from you.*"
> [WORD of GOD in Genesis 17:6]

Apart from the above reasons, any who still feel that heaven rather than earth will be the location of God's Kingdom, need to also explain away the following Biblical points:[78]

The 'Lord's Prayer' asks for God's Kingdom to come (as they pray for the return of Christ), asking that God's desires will be done on earth as they are now done in heaven.[79]

---

[78] Adapted from *The Place Of Reward: Heaven Or Earth?* http://www.christadelphians.com/ biblebasics/ 0407 theplaceofreward.html

[79] Matthew 6:10

We are therefore praying for God's Kingdom to come on the earth. It is a tragedy that thousands of people thoughtlessly pray these words each day still believing that God's Kingdom is now already fully established in heaven, and that the earth will be totally destroyed.

"Blessed are the gentle (meek): for they shall inherit the **earth**" (Matthew 5:5) – the Biblical text does not say '...for their souls shall go to heaven'.

This is alluding to Psalm 37, the whole of which emphasizes that the final reward of the righteous will be upon the earth.[80]

In the very same location that the wicked had enjoyed their temporary supremacy, the righteous will be recompensed with eternal life, and possess this same earth that the wicked once dominated.

"The humble shall inherit the **earth**...Those who are blessed by him shall inherit the earth...The righteous shall inherit the land [earth], and dwell in it permanently".[81] Living *in* the earth/promised land permanently (forever) means that eternal life in heaven is an impossibility.

---

[80] Psalm 37:29, 34-36 [emphasis added]
[81] Psalm 37:11,22,29 [emphasis added]

Millennial Kingdom of God on Planet Earth

"David...is both dead and buried...David is not ascended into the heavens" (Acts 2:29,34). Instead, Peter explained that his hope was the resurrection from the dead at Christ's return (Acts 2:22-36).

Earth is the arena of God's operations with mankind: "The heavens, are the Lord's, but the **earth** He has given to the human race".[82]

Revelation 5:9-10 relates a vision of what the righteous will say when they are accepted at the judgment seat: "(Christ) hath made us to our God priests: and we will reign on the earth".

This picture of ruling in God's Kingdom on earth is quite removed from the vague conception that we will enjoy 'bliss' somewhere in heaven.

The prophecies of Daniel chapters 2 and 7 outline a succession of political powers, which will ultimately be superseded by the Kingdom of God at Christ's return.

The dominion of this Kingdom would fill "the whole *earth*"[83] and never be destroyed.[84]

---

[82] Psalm 115:16 [emphasis added]
[83] Daniel **7:27**; Daniel **2:35**
[84] Daniel 2:44

This everlasting Kingdom "will be given to the people - the holy ones of the most High";[85] their reward is therefore eternal life in this Kingdom which is to be located **on earth**, *under* the heavens.

Presently, however, only those whom God calls and works with have voluntarily submitted to God's rule. These people, known as Faithful Followers of Jesus, the Messiah, have been born again—spiritually regenerated as a new creation—into a relationship with God and Christ and have become heirs to the Kingdom of God.[86]

Paul writes that "our citizenship is in heaven, from which we also eagerly wait for the Savior, the Lord Jesus Christ".[87]

He likens us to "ambassadors for Christ",[88] emissaries of a foreign government, subject to its laws and methods.

However, these Faithful Followers [Believing Christians] have not yet fully entered into God's Kingdom; they are still flesh and blood, which "cannot inherit the kingdom of God".[89]

---

[85] Daniel 7:27
[86] **see** Ephesians 2:5-7
[87] Philippians 3:20
[88] 2nd Corinthians 5:20
[89] 1st Corinthians 15:50

Millennial Kingdom of God on Planet Earth

This entry will occur at the resurrection from the dead when Christ returns to this earth to restore God's government, bringing peace and prosperity to all.[90]

The Kingdom of God will then be a real, physical entity on the earth, ruled by Jesus Christ with the help of His brethren, the resurrected, immortal saints.[91]

Christ will come *from* heaven to be with us, rather than the other way around.

Where did the idea that heaven is the reward of the saved originate?
Does the Old Testament teach it? No.
Did Jesus and His apostles teach it?[92] No.

The doctrine originated with the pagan, polytheistic Greeks and Romans. Their deified heroes and other favorites of their multiple gods were supposedly given admission to their "heaven," which they called "Elysium."

Various peoples evolved their own versions of Elysium.
The Germans and Scandinavians had their Valhalla.

---

[90] **Isaiah 9:6-7; Acts 3:19-21; 1ˢᵗ Corinthians 15:22-28**
[91] **Revelation 5:10, 20:4-6**
[92] Adapted from https://www.cgg.org/index.cfm/fuseaction/Library.sr/CT/RA/k/848/Is-Heaven-Reward-of-Saved.htm

The American Indians had their Happy Hunting Grounds.

The eastern Buddhists have Nirvana, which offers the dubious promise of "the extinction of all desire and personality."

The Western, man-originated "heaven" is more similar to the original Greek concept.

Prophets told of the Kingdom's Location

What then does the Bible further teach about the location of God's Kingdom and the reward of his Faithful Followers?

Verses 44-45 of Daniel chapter 2 provide:
> In the days of those kings, the God of heaven will set up a kingdom that will never be destroyed, and this kingdom will not be left to another people.
> It will crush all these kingdoms and bring them to an end, but will itself endure forever. You saw a stone break off from the mountain without a hand touching it, and it crushed the iron, bronze, fired clay, silver, and gold.
> The great God has told the king what will happen in the future.
> The dream is true, and its interpretation certain.

Millennial Kingdom of God on Planet Earth

**These verses say that God's Kingdom will encompass all of the previous kingdoms—on earth!
Daniel 7:17-18 says much the same.**

And, Daniel 7:27 adds a vital piece of information concerning our understanding of where God's Kingdom will be:
> **Then the sovereignty, the dominion, and the greatness of *all* the kingdoms under the whole heaven will be given to the people of the saints of the Highest One; His kingdom *will be* an everlasting kingdom, and all the empires will serve and obey Him.[93]**

**God's everlasting Kingdom shall not be in heaven but "*under* the whole heaven"!
Why then should we be surprised that God's Kingdom will be on earth?**

God tells us through Moses that ancient Israel was a type of God's Kingdom and, in fact, could have been His Kingdom had they obeyed Him:
> **Now if you will listen to Me and carefully keep My covenant, you will be My own possession out of all the peoples, although all the earth is Mine, and you will be My kingdom of priests and My holy nation.[94]**

---

[93] Daniel 7:27 [New American Standard Bible 2020}
[94] Exodus 19:5-6

And, in the "Lord's Prayer," which many repeat every day: "Your kingdom come. Your will be done on earth as it is in heaven",[95] Jesus instructs His Faithful Followers to pray for God's Kingdom to *come to earth*, not to be taken away to Heaven!

Obadiah verses 17 and 21 specifically tell us where God's Kingdom will be set up:
> But there will be a deliverance on Mount Zion,
> and it will be holy;
> the house of Jacob will dispossess
> those who dispossessed them.
>
> Those who have been delivered will ascend
> Mount Zion to rule over the hill country of Esau,
> but the Kingdom will be the Lord's.

Likewise, Micah 4:1-2 shows that Jesus Christ will dwell on earth in Jerusalem, accessible to physical people and nations:
> In the last days the mountain of the Lord's
> house will be established at the top of the
> mountains and will be raised above the hills.
>
> Peoples will stream to it,
> and many nations will come and say,
> "Come, let us go up to the mountain of the Lord,
> to the house of the God of Jacob.

---

[95] Matthew 6:10; also see Micah 4:8

Millennial Kingdom of God on Planet Earth

> **He will teach us about His ways**
> **so we may walk in His paths."**
>
> **For instruction will go out of Zion**
> **and the word of the Lord from Jerusalem.**

And, Matthew 24:3 shows that the disciples knew, and therefore were taught by Jesus Himself, that He would come back to this earth, when they asked Him, "Tell us, when will these things be? And what will be the sign of Your coming, and of the end of the age?"

In His reply, Jesus continually repeats that He will *come back* to this earth:

> **For as the lightning comes from the east and**
> **flashes as far as the west, so will be the coming**
> **of the Son of Man.**[96]
> **Immediately after the tribulation of those days:**
> **The sun will be darkened, and the moon**
> **will not shed its light; the stars will fall**
> **from the sky, and the celestial powers will**
> **be shaken.**
> **Then the sign of the Son of Man will**
> **appear in the sky, and then all the peoples**
> **of the earth will mourn; and they will see**
> **the Son of Man coming on the clouds of heaven**
> **with power and great glory.** [97]

---

[96] Matthew 24:27
[97] Matthew 24:2-30

Now concerning that day and hour no one knows—neither the angels in heaven, nor the Son — except the Father only. As the days of Noah were, so the coming of the Son of Man will be.[98]

This is why you also must be ready, because the Son of Man is coming at an hour you do not expect.[99]
(see also Matthew 24 verses 39, 42, 44, 46, 48, 50)

Some may argue that, because Jesus went to be with God the Father in heaven after his death and resurrection, we must go to heaven to be with him.

But, the disciples, after all of Jesus' teaching, despite being still limited in their knowledge and understanding, knew for sure that Jesus was to restore His Kingdom to Israel.[100]

The Disciples' understanding of Jesus' future Second Coming was enhanced by the event recorded in Acts 1:9-11:
> After He [Jesus] had said this, He was taken up as they were watching, and a cloud took Him out of their sight.

---

[98] Matthew 24:36-37
[99] Matthew 24:44
[100] Acts 1:6

> While He was going, they were gazing into heaven, and suddenly two men in white clothes stood by them.
> They said, "Men of Galilee, why do you stand looking up into heaven? This Jesus, who has been taken from you into heaven, will come in the same way that you have seen Him going into heaven.

At his Second Coming, Jesus will come down from heaven, through the clouds, first to Bozrah/Petra[101] and them make his victory ascent up the Mount of Olives just outside Jerusalem.[102]

He will be clearly visible to human eyes.

Christ reveals to the apostle John in Revelation 19:11-21 that He will not return meekly or unnoticed to this earth. His return will be witnessed by the whole world whose kings and armies (verse 19) will gather to battle against Him- during the Campaign of Armageddon.

1st Thessalonians 4:17 says that we are to be with the Lord forever, but where will the Lord be?
Again, many scriptures give the answer, but Zechariah 14:4 gives a clear and concise answer:
> On that day His feet will stand on the Mount

---

[101] Isaiah 63:1-6, Isaiah 34:1-7, Habakkuk 3:3, and Micah 2:12-13.
[102] Zechariah 14:4

of Olives, which faces Jerusalem on the east. The Mount of Olives will be split in half from east to west, forming a huge valley, so that half the mountain will move to the north and half to the south.

This is not some "heavenly" Mount of Olives! It is the literal one on Planet Earth which faces Jerusalem on the east!
Nor is it a "spiritual" Jerusalem; rather it is an actual mountain which Jesus is going to split in half!

At Jesus' Second Coming to earth who will be with Him? The second half of Zechariah 14:5 [NASB] informs us: "Thus the Lord my God will come, and all the holy ones with Him ."

Will He stay on earth after his Second Coming? Notice Zechariah 14:9:
    And the Lord will be king over all the earth.
    On that day there will be one Lord—
    his name alone will be worshiped.[103]

Yes, He will stay. The Kingdom of God and the reward of his Faithful Followers are on this earth! As Jesus Himself tells us in Matthew 5:5, "Blessed are the gentle (meek): for they shall inherit the earth."

---

[103] Zechariah 14:9 [New Living Translation]

Millennial Kingdom of God on Planet Earth

The biblical record is plain: God's Kingdom will be established on the earth He created, and it will be an everlasting Kingdom.

For additional Biblical Texts concerning the Kingdom of God being established on earth, see
    Psalm 2:6-8; 47:1-9; Jeremiah 23:5;
    Ezekiel 37:21-28; Daniel 2:44-45;
    Daniel 7:17-18, 27; Micah 4:1-5;
    Zechariah 2:19-12; 8:3; 9:9-10; 14:9, 16-17; and
    Revelation 2:26-27.

Chapter Seven
Jesus Will Be the King

There can be no doubt that the *King* of God's Kingdom will be Jesus of Nazareth, the Messiah.[104] Even though Jesus did not exercise any civil authority while on earth, when He returns as promised he will be King of kings and Lord of lords.[105]

And as promised, Jesus will come again to earth, this time with His saints and with His army of angels too. He will take His rightful place on His glorious, earthly throne and share power with His saints over the physical nations of the earth.[106]

As shown previously[107], one of the basic elements of the Kingdom of God is Royal Authority: status as a member of the Holy Trinity: God the Father, God the Son or the Holy Spirit.

David, one of ancient Israel's greatest kings, was well aware that his [David's] physical kingdom of Israel was only a type of the Kingdom that God would later establish.

---

[104] Adapted from *Who Will Be King?*, retrieved at www.truegospel.org/index.cfm/fuseaction/basics.tour/ID/3/Who-Will-Be-King.htm

[105] 1st Timothy 6:15; Revelation 19:16 and 17:14. See also Psalm 2:7-9.

[106] See Psalm 2:8-9; Revelation 2:26-27; Revelation 19:11-15; Matthew 24:30

[107] *Supra*, Chapter 3 hereof.

David recognized the coming Royal Authority: **God, the Son, will be the King** over the earth and all of its inhabitants.[108] Jesus will be given the nations for his inheritance, and the ends of the earth for his possession. He will be King forever and ever.[109]

When that Kingdom is established, all the ends of the world shall remember and turn to the LORD, and all the families of the nations shall worship before him. The kingdom is the LORD's, and he rules over the nations.[110]

However, while the LORD God Almighty is sovereign over all the earth, it is also painfully obvious to us today as we survey the world around us that this prophecy of the world turning to the Lord has yet to be fulfilled.

The LORD God Almighty made promises and through his prophets recorded prophecies about the coming King as far back as the time of Abraham time.[111] God later repeats this promise of royal offspring to Abraham's grandson, Jacob.[112]

His prophecy through Jacob to his sons also predicts a

---

[108] Psalm 2:6-8; 110:1
[109] Psalm 2:8-9; 10:16; 29:10; 45:6; 145:13
[110] Psalm 22:27-28; Philippians 2:10
[111] Genesis 17:6
[112] Genesis 35:11

coming King, saying of Judah, " The scepter will not depart from Judah, nor the ruler's staff from between his feet, until Shiloh comes, And to him *shall be* the obedience of the peoples.[113]

Centuries later, the LORD God Almighty inspires Balaam to prophesy: "I see him, but not now; I perceive him, but not near. A star shall come out of Jacob, and a scepter shall rise out of Israel. ... One who comes from Jacob One will rule".[114]

Other prophets also foretold of a coming King, not just of Israel and Judah, but also extending to the entire world.

Isaiah tells us:
> For a child will be born for us,
> a son will be given to us,
> and the **government** will be on
>   his shoulders.
> He will be named
> Wonderful Counselor, Mighty God,
> Eternal Father, Prince of Peace.
> The dominion will be vast,
> and its prosperity will never end.
> He will reign on the **throne of David**
> and over his kingdom,

---

[113] Genesis 49:10 [NASB]
[114] Numbers 24:17, 19

to establish and sustain it
with justice and righteousness from now on and forever.
The zeal of the Lord of Armies will accomplish this.[115]

Similarly, Jeremiah writes,
Look, the days are coming—this is the Lord's declaration—
when I will raise up a Righteous Branch for David.
He will reign wisely as king
and administer justice and righteousness in the land.
In his days Judah will be saved,
and Israel will dwell securely.
This is the name he will be called:
The Lord Is Our Righteousness.[116]

And the prophet Micah foretold that the Messiah coming out of Bethlehem, would be the One to be ruler over Israel – and included that his greatness will extend to the ends of the earth.[117]

Accordingly, when, on Palm Sunday, the people saw Jesus entering Jerusalem on a donkey[118], some recognized it as a fulfillment of Zechariah 9:9:
Rejoice greatly, Daughter Zion!

---

[115] Isaiah 9:6-7 [emphasis added]
[116] Jeremiah 23:5-6
[117] Micah 5:2-4
[118] Matthew 21:2-9

> Shout in triumph, Daughter Jerusalem!
> Look, your King is coming to you;
> he is righteous and victorious,
> humble and riding on a donkey,
> on a colt, the foal of a donkey.

When Jesus came to earth the first time, he came as a *messenger* rather than as a *ruler.*[119]

Jesus came to deliver the Good News about His coming Kingdom, but that Kingdom will not be fully established on Planet Earth until His Second Coming when all nations shall come and worship before him, their King.[120]

At his first coming Jesus proclaimed the Good News about his coming Kingdom, but as we look at world conditions today it is painfully obvious that the prophecy of the world turning to Jesus has yet to be fulfilled.

This same King, the "First and the Last",[121] who entered Jerusalem on a donkey two thousand years ago will not establish his Millennial Kingdom on planet Earth until his Second Coming when all nations shall come and worship Him, their King.[122]

---

[119] Malachi 3:1. Also see John 6:15.
[120] Revelation 15:3-4
[121] Isaiah 44:6; Revelation 1:17; 2:8; 22:13
[122] Zechariah 14:16; see Revelation 15:3. See Zechariah 14:9.

Millennial Kingdom of God on Planet Earth

Yet, in a way, Jesus Christ has already fulfilled parts of these prophecies because He was born to be and is a King.[123]

Jesus of Nazareth, the Messiah, will return to planet Earth:
- **Personally,**[124]
- **Bodily (not just as a spirit),**[125]
- **Visibly,**[126]
- **Suddenly,**[127]
- **Dramatically,**[128]
- **Gloriously,**[129] and
- **Triumphantly as King of Kings and LORD of Lords**[130]

And, this Jesus He's my King too!

Have You Met My King?[131]

My King was born King.
The Bible says He's a 7-Way King.
>   He's the King of the Jews - that's an Ethnic King.

---

[123] Matthew 2:2-7; 21:4-5; 27:11; Luke 1:30-33; John 12:13-16; 18:36-37; Acts 17:7
[124] Acts 1:11
[125] Acts 1:9-11
[126] Revelation 1:7
[127] Matthew 24:27
[128] Matthew 24:29-30; Luke 21:25-28
[129] Matthew 24:30; 2nd Thessalonians 1:7
[130] Revelation 19:16; Matthew 19:28; Luke 1:32-33; Isaiah 9:6-7. See Daniel 2:44
[131] Adapted from Detroit 1976 sermon by Dr. S.M. Lockeridge of San Diego, CA.

He's the King of Israel - that's a National King.
He's the King of righteousness.
He's the King of the ages.
He's the King of Heaven.
He's the King of glory.
He's the King of kings and the Lord of lords.
   Now that's my King.

Do you know Him?
Do you know my King?

He's enduringly strong.
He's entirely sincere.
He's eternally steadfast.
He's immortally graceful.
He's imperially powerful.
He's impartially merciful.

That's my King. He's God's Son.

He's the sinner's savior.
He's the centerpiece of civilization.
He's honest.
He's unique.
He's unparalleled.
He's unprecedented.
He's pre-eminent.
He's supreme.

Millennial Kingdom of God on Planet Earth

He's the grandest idea in literature.
He's the highest personality in philosophy.
He's the supreme problem in higher criticism.
He's the fundamental doctrine of historic theology.
He's the necessity of spiritual religion.
   That's my King.

He's the miracle of the ages.
He's the superlative of everything good that you choose to call Him. He's the only one able to supply all our needs simultaneously.
He supplies strength for the weak.
He's available for the tempted and the tried.
He sympathizes and He saves.
He's the Almighty God who guides and keeps all his people.

He heals the sick.
He cleanses.
He forgives sinners.
He delivers the captives.
He defends the feeble.
He serves the unfortunate.
He blesses the young.
He regards the aged.
He rewards the diligent and He beautifies the meek.
   That's my King.

Do you know Him?

Well, my King is a King of knowledge.
He's the wellspring of wisdom.
He's the doorway of deliverance.
He's the pathway of peace.
He's the roadway of righteousness.
He's the highway of holiness.
He's the gateway of glory.
He's the master of the mighty.
He's the captain of the conquerors.
He's the head of the heroes.
He's the leader of the legislatures.
He's the overseer of the Overcomers.
He's the governor of governors.
He's the prince of princes.
He's the King of kings and He's the Lord of lords.
   That's my King.

His office is manifold.
His promise is sure.
His light is matchless.
His goodness is limitless.
His mercy is everlasting.
His love never changes.
His Word is enough.
His grace is sufficient.
His reign is righteous.
His yoke is easy and His burden is light.
I wish I could describe Him to you . . . but He's indescribable.

Millennial Kingdom of God on Planet Earth

That's my King.

He's incomprehensible, He's invincible, and He is irresistible.

The heavens can't contain Him, let alone some man explain Him. You can't get Him out of your mind.
You can't get Him off of your hands.
You can't outlive Him and
    you can't live without Him.

The Pharisees couldn't stand Him, but they couldn't stop Him.
Pilate couldn't find any fault in Him.
The witnesses couldn't get their testimonies to agree about Him.
Herod couldn't kill Him.
Death couldn't handle Him and the grave couldn't hold Him.
    That's my King.
He always has been and He always will be.
He had no predecessor and He'll have no successor.
There's nobody before Him;
    there'll be nobody after Him.
You can't impeach Him and He's not going to resign.
    That's my King! - my King!

All the power belongs to my King.
His is the kingdom and the power and the glory.

We talk about black power and white power and yellow power,
but in the end all that matters is God's power.
Thine is the power.
   And the glory.
   The glory is all His.

Thine is the Kingdom and the power and glory,
   forever and ever and ever and ever.
How long is that?
   Forever and ever and ever and
      ever...
And when you get through with all of the forever's,
   then ... Amen!

That's My King !!

Millennial Kingdom of God on Planet Earth

Chapter 8
When will the Kingdom of God be Established?

No one on Earth knows the specific day of the Second Coming of the Messiah.

Scripture tells us:
> Now concerning that day and hour no one knows—
> neither the angels in heaven, nor the Son —
> except the Father only. As the days of Noah were, so the coming of the Son of Man will be.[132]
>
> This is why you also must be ready, because the Son of Man is coming at an hour you do not expect.[133]

But, the Holy Scriptures do inform us of the chain of End Time events during the coming Day of the LORD.[134]

---

[132] Matthew 24:36-37
[133] Matthew 24:44. See also Matthew 24:39, 42, 46, 50.
[134] See Bob Chadwick, *Understanding the Day of the LORD* , . End-Times Library, vol. 001.

Millennial Kingdom of God on Planet Earth

The following End Time events will occur before Jesus' return to establish his Kingdom on Earth:
1. **Anti-Christ revealed and signs Peace Pact with Israel;**[135]
2. **Seven-year Tribulation period;**[136]
3. **Abomination of Desolation occurs in rebuilt Temple in Jerusalem;**[137]
4. **Jerusalem falls again into Gentile hands;**[138] **and most importantly,**
5. **The surviving Remnant of Jews recognize Jesus of Nazareth as their LORD and Savior and plead for his Second Coming.**[139]

Soon after the Remnant recognizes Jesus and pleads for his return, Jesus will return to Planet Earth to rescue the Remnant, defeat Satan, the Anti-Christ and his armies and establish his Millennial Kingdom on Earth.

---

[135] Daniel 9:27; Revelation 13:1-8
[136] Daniel 9:27 [Amplified Bible, New Century Version & the Living Bible]
[137] Daniel 9:27; Matthew 24:15-22; 2nd Thessalonians 2:3-10
[138] Zechariah 14:1-2
[139] Leviticus 26:39-42; Jeremiah 3:12-18; Hosea 5:15-6:3; Zechariah 12:10-13:1; Matthew 23:37-39

With Jesus as he returns will be the armies of heaven and his Faithful Followers who had been previously raptured before the Tribulation.[140]

THE 75-DAY INTERVAL PERIOD

The Millennial Kingdom of Jesus of Nazareth, the Messiah, does not begin immediately after the end of the 7-year Tribulation.[141]

The 7-year Tribulation is divided into a 1260-day first half (3 ½ years) and a 1260-day second half (called the Great Tribulation or Time of Jacob's Trouble).[142]

The event that signals the beginning of the second half of the Tribulation period will be the Anti-Christ's takeover of the Jewish Temple from which he will declare himself to be God. The Anti-Christ will then have the False Prophet set up his image in the Temple, thus committing the Abomination of Desolation.

Jesus of Nazareth, the Messiah, will return to Planet Earth at the end of the 7-year Tribulation. `

Thereafter a seventy-five-day interval will intervene

---

[140] Zechariah 14:5; Matthew25:31; 1st Thessalonians 3:13; 2nd Thessalonians 1:7; Jude 1:14; Revelation 19:14. Dr. Arnold G. Fruchtenbaum, *Footsteps of the Messiah*, p.346.
[141] Dr, Arnold Fruchtenbaum, *Footsteps of the Messiah*, p. 361
[142] Jeremiah 30:7; see Matthew 24:4-19; *Israel My Glory*, May/June 2005.

Millennial Kingdom of God on Planet Earth

between the end of the Great Tribulation and the commencement of the Messianic Millennium.[143]

EVENTS DURING 75-DAY INTERVAL[144]

1. Removal of the Abomination of Desolation[145]

It will take 30 days for the idol of the Anti-Christ to be removed from the rebuilt Tribulation Temple and the temple cleansed.[146] The Bible does not indicate why that Abomination of Desolation is permitted to continue thirty days beyond the end of the Tribulation.

This Tribulation Temple will ultimately be replaced by the Messianic Millennium Temple.[147]

2. Binding Satan for 1,000 Years[148]

Scripture informs us that Satan, will be bound and cast, for a thousand years, into the abyss (section of Sheol/Hades that is a temporary place of confinement for fallen angels).[149]

---

[143] Daniel 12:11-12; also see Daniel 12:5-10, 13.
The Tribulation ends 1,260 days after the midpoint of the Tribulation.
The Millennial Kingdom begins 1,335 days after the midpoint of the Tribulation. Thus, there is a transitional interval period of seventy-five days from the end of the Tribulation until the commencement of the Kingdom (1,335 minus 1,260).

[144] Adapted from Ariel Staff, the Seventy-five Day Interval, retrieved at http://arielb.org/archives/774.

[145] Daniel 12:11

[146] *Ibid.*

[147] Dr. Arnold G. Fruchtenbaum, MBS042-*The Seventy-five Day Interval*, p.5. See Ezekiel, chapters 40-42.

[148] Revelation 20:1-3

[149] Dr. Arnold G. Fruchtenbaum, MBS042-*The Seventy-five Day Interval*, p.6.

3. Judgment of Gentile Nations: Sheep and Goats[150]

This judgment is described in two passages of scripture: Joel chapter 3 and Matthew 25:31-46 and takes place after the end of the tribulation period but prior to the Millennium. The purpose of the Judgment of the Gentile Nations is to determine who will enter the Millennial Kingdom.

Scripture in Joel 3 provides the basis for the Judgment of the Gentile Nations including the location and timing:

> Yes, in those days and at that time, [*End-Times*] when I [J<u>e</u>hovah] restore the fortunes of Judah and Jerusalem,
> I will gather all the nations and take them to the Valley of Jehoshaphat.
> I will enter into judgment with them there because of My people, My inheritance Israel.
>
> The nations have scattered the Israelites in foreign countries and divided up My land.
> They cast lots for My people; they bartered a boy for a prostitute and sold a girl for wine to drink.
>   [WORD of GOD in Joel 3:1-3 emphasis added]

Also Matthew 25:31-46 is interpreted as referring to the Judgment of the Nations:

> But when the Son of Man comes in his glory,

---
[150] Matthew 25:31-46

Millennial Kingdom of God on Planet Earth

and all the holy angels with him, then he will
sit on the throne of his glory.

Before him all the nations will be gathered, and
he will separate them one from another, as a
shepherd separates the sheep from the goats.
He will set the sheep on his right hand, but
the goats on the left.

Then the King will tell those on his right hand,
'Come, blessed of my Father, inherit the Kingdom
prepared for you from the foundation of the world
    for I was hungry, and you gave me food to eat.
    I was thirsty, and you gave me drink.
    I was a stranger, and you took me in.
    I was naked, and you clothed me.
    I was sick, and you visited me.
    I was in prison, and you came to me.' …

The King will answer them, 'Most certainly
I tell you, because you did it to one of the least
of these my brothers, you did it to me.'

Then he will say also to those on the left hand,
'Depart from me, you cursed, into the eternal
fire which is prepared for the devil and his angels;
for I was hungry, and you didn't give me food
    to eat;
I was thirsty, and you gave me no drink;

> I was a stranger, and you didn't take me in;
> naked, and you didn't clothe me;
> sick, and in prison, and you didn't visit me.'...
>
> These will go away into eternal punishment,
>   but the righteous into eternal life.
>   [WORD of GOD in Matthew 25:31-46]

The nations are comprised of the sheep and the goats, representing the saved and the lost among the Gentiles.

According to Matthew 25:32, they are intermingled and require separation by a special judgment.
This judgment follows the second coming of Christ, since it occurs "when the Son of Man comes in his glory, and all the holy angels with him".[151]

Although some would argue[152] that the judgment of the Sheep and the Goats in Matthew 25 is the same as the Great White Throne Judgment of Revelation 20:11-15, a close reading of the applicable Holy Scriptures makes that view unlikely:

• Different Time: The judgment of the nations occurs at the second coming of Christ (Matthew 25:31) whereas the Great White Throne Judgment occurs following the end of the 1,000-year Messianic Millennial Kingdom (Revelation 20:11-12).

---

[151] Adapted from Dr. Ron Rhodes, *Posttribulationism and the Sheep/Goat-Judgment of Matthew 25*, p.1.
[152] See Robert Gundry, *The Church and the Tribulation*.

Millennial Kingdom of God on Planet Earth

- **Different Subjects:** At the judgment of the nations, three groups of people are mentioned: the sheep, the goats, and the brothers (Matthew 25:32, 40) whereas the Great White Throne judgment involves the unsaved dead (Revelation 20:12).

- **Different Basis:** The basis of judgment at the judgment of the nations is how Christ's "brothers" were treated (Matthew 25:40) whereas the basis of judgment at the Great White Throne is the works of the unsaved dead (Revelation 20:12).

- **Different Result:** The result of the judgment of the nations is twofold: the righteous enter into the Messianic Millennial kingdom; the unrighteous are cast into the lake of fire.

The result of the Great White Throne judgment is that the wicked dead are cast into the lake of fire (the righteous are not mentioned).

- **Resurrection:** No resurrection is mentioned in connection with the judgment of the nations.
A resurrection of the dead does take place in connection with the Great White Throne judgment (Revelation 20:13).

WHO ARE THE NATIONS MENTIONED IN MATTHEW 25:32 AND JOEL 3:2?

The term "nations" (Greek *ethnē*) is used in the New Testament in both a broad universal sense: *all the nations on planet earth*[153], or a narrower sense: *Gentiles or "non-Jewish people"*[154] with the context of the particular passage of Scripture indicating the proper translation.[155]

This compiler agrees with Drs. Fruchtenbaum and Rhodes that in the context of Matthew 25:32, the term "nations" refers to non-Jewish Gentiles.[156]

And our opinion is confirmed by Joel 3:2 where the context clearly indicates that the Hebrew word (*gōwyim*), translated "nations" refers to a foreign nation composed of non-Jewish Gentiles.[157]

As Dr. Rhodes concludes, the view that "all the

---

[153] See Stanley Toussaint, *Behold the King: A Study of Matthew* (Portland, OR: Multnomah Press, 1980), p. 290.

[154] William F. Arndt and F. Wilbur Gingrich, *A Greek-English Lexicon of the New Testament and Other Early Christian Literature* (Chicago, IL: University of Chicago Press, 1957), p. 217.

[155] Walter Edman, *"The Judgment of the Gentiles,"* Th.M. Thesis, Dallas Theological Seminary, 1980, p. 44.

[156] Dr. Arnold G. Fruchtenbaum, *Footsteps of the Messiah*, p. 365; Dr. Ron Rhodes, *Posttribulationism and the Sheep/Goat- Judgment of Matthew 25*, p. 3.

[157] Notice that in Joel 3:2 "all the nations" are distinct from the Jews who are referred to as "My people and My inheritance, Israel". See also Strong's *Exhaustive Concordance of the Bible*, Hebrew 1471 where the root *gōwy* is defined as a foreign *nation,* hence a non-Jewish *Gentile.*

nations" refers to living Gentiles who survive the tribulation period is substantiated by etymological studies, the context of the book of Matthew, Old Testament prophecy in Joel and the Abrahamic covenant (I will bless those who bless you, I will curse those who treat you with contempt).[158]

Timing of the Judgment of the Nations

The Judgment of the Nations will occur in the End-Times during the 75-day interval between the Second Coming of the Messiah and the beginning of the Messianic Millennium after the national regeneration of Israel and the true destiny of Judah and Jerusalem has been restored.[159]

PLACE WHERE THE JUDGMENT OF THE NATIONS OCCURS

The Judgment of the Nations will occur in the Valley of Jehoshaphat (also known as the Kidron Valley) in Jerusalem.[160] The Valley of Jehoshaphat is on the east side of the city of Jerusalem and separates the Temple Mount from the Mount of Olives.

---

[158] Genesis 12:3. Dr. Ron Rhodes, *Posttribulationism and the Sheep/Goat-Judgment of Matthew 25*, p. 6.
[159] Joel 3:1. See Chapter 6 hereof *supra*, at Phase 6. National Regeneration of Israel.
[160] Joel 3:2

This was the same place where the Campaign of Armageddon will end.

REASON FOR THE JUDGMENT OF THE NATIONS

The gentile nations will be judged as to whether or not their actions were anti-Semitic including whether the gentiles concerned had scattered the Jewish people to foreign countries, sold them into slavery or divided up the Jewish land.[161]

The indictment against the nations of the world is that they have participated in the partition of God's land. Such partition will bring judgment to the nations involved.

The land of Israel is not the property of the United Nations, the Vatican, the European Union nor the Arabs. Neither is it the property of Israel, for it belongs to God himself.[162]

The LORD God Almighty spoke to the Jewish People through Moses:
> The land [Israel] is not to be permanently sold because **it is Mine**, and you are only foreigners and temporary residents on My land.
> [WORD of GOD in Leviticus 25:23 emphasis added]

---

[161] Joel 3:2-3, 12; Matthew 25:32
[162] Pastor Bill Randles, *God Sues the Nations Joel 3 – Part 1* retrieved at http://www.believersingrace.com/joel3part1.html

Millennial Kingdom of God on Planet Earth

[Compiler: *This Biblical text still remains true today, even though the strict Mosaic law was done away with on the Cross, because it pertains to God's ownership, not that of the Jews.*]

Not even the Jews have the right to trade land for peace, although it appears the leadership of Israel, being for the most part secular in their outlook, would desperately love to do so if it would bring peace.

Accordingly, for the nations of the world to deliberate at the United Nations or elsewhere as to the disposal of the Holy Land and its borders, as if it were theirs to dispose of, is an "arrogant presumption".[163]

WHAT KINGDOM IS REFERRED TO IN MATTHEW 25:34

Dr. Lewis Chafer writes with reference to Matthew 25:34, "There is no reason why the word kingdom should be given any other meaning in this passage than has been assigned to it throughout the Gospel by Matthew. The kingdom is Israel's earthly, Messianic, millennial kingdom".[164]

Matthew's Gospel is intimately related to the Abrahamic and Davidic covenants. The Abrahamic

---

[163] *Ibid.*
[164] Lewis Sperry Chafer, *Systematic Theology*, (Dallas, TX: Dallas Seminary Press, 1948), 5:137

and Davidic covenants are two of four unconditional covenants made by the LORD God Almighty with the Jewish people These covenants come into view in Matthew's genealogy which begins with the words, "The book of the genealogy of Jesus Christ, the son of David, the son of Abraham."

Matthew, in beginning his Gospel this way, highlights that Jesus came to fulfill the Covenants made with Israel's forefathers[165] and institute the Messianic Millennial kingdom foretold in the Davidic covenant.[166]

WHO ARE MY BROTHERS OF MATTHEW 25:40?
"The nations" of Matthew 25:32 are made up of *only* the sheep and the goats. Accordingly, the brothers of Matthew 25:40 are distinct from the nations (or Gentiles).
Therefore, the "brothers" of Matthew 25:40 must be made up of Christ's brothers *after the flesh*— redeemed Jews. [167]

---

[165] See Charles L. Feinberg, "The Eternal Kingship of Christ," in *Jesus the King Is Coming* (Chicago, IL: Moody Press, 1975), p. 185.
[166] See Toussaint, *Behold the King: A Study of Matthew*, p. 289. Dr. Ron Rhodes, *Posttribulationism and the Sheep/Goat-Judgment of Matthew 25*, p.8.
[167] See Dr. Ron Rhodes, *Posttribulationism and the Sheep/Goat-Judgment of Matthew 25*, p. 11.

Millennial Kingdom of God on Planet Earth

Chapter 9
Who are the Kingdom's Subjects and Citizens?

A Kingdom has both subjects and citizens. Even though the entire world will be ruled by Jesus Christ when He establishes the Kingdom on Earth, not everyone on earth will be a *citizen* of that Kingdom.

Everyone will be *subject* to the King of kings, but not everyone will have entered as a citizen into that spiritual Kingdom.

Scripture makes in plain that there will be human, animal and plant inhabitants.

A. Human Inhabitants[168]
The human inhabitants of the Kingdom fall into three groups:
- God's people on earth at Tribulation's close,
- those returned alive to earth during the 75-day Interval period and
- those who are born into the Kingdom.

---

[168] Adapted from Norman Manzon, *The Inhabitants of the Kingdom, p.1-9*

Millennial Kingdom of God on Planet Earth

1. GOD'S PEOPLE ON EARTH AT THE END OF THE TRIBULATION

God's people on earth at the end of the Tribulation will be Jesus Himself, those who accompanied Jesus at his return, the saved Jewish Remnant and the "sheep" Gentiles.

a. THE LORD JESUS

The LORD Jesus will remain on earth into the Kingdom Age to once again "tabernacle" or dwell among us just as He did at His first coming.

The Apostle John wrote concerning Jesus' First Coming:
> The Word became flesh and dwelt [Greek: *tented, tabernacled*] among us. We observed his glory, the glory as the one and only Son from the Father, full of grace and truth.
> [WORD of GOD in John 1:14]

Jesus' presence during the Millennial Kingdom will be the ultimate fulfillment of the annual Mosaic Feast of Tabernacles.[169]

---

[169] Leviticus 23:33-44; Amos 9:11; Zechariah 14:16

b. Those Who Accompanied Jesus

The raptured Faithful Followers will return to earth with the Lord[170] and remain on earth for duration of the Kingdom Age.

c. Remnant of Jews Saved During the Tribulation

The Remnant is the one-third of Israel who remain alive at Tribulation's end. It is comprised of the 144,000 Israelite witnesses of Revelation 7 and those Jews who will receive Jesus as Messiah at the end of the Tribulation.

d. The "Sheep" Gentiles

The "sheep" are those Gentiles who receive the Lord during the Tribulation and display their regenerated state by assisting the Jews whom the Anti-Christ was trying to annihilate.

They differ from the other saved survivors of the Tribulation because before their entry into the Kingdom they must first undergo the Judgment of the Sheep and Goats a test which all the sheep pass.[171]

---

[170] Jude 1:14
[171] Matthew 25:34-40; see end of Chapter 8 hereof, *supra*.

Millennial Kingdom of God on Planet Earth

2. Those Returned Alive to Earth During the 75-day Interval Period

As noted in Chapter 8, *supra*, a seventy-five day interval will intervene between the end of the Great Tribulation and the commencement of the Messianic Millennium.[172]

This group is comprised of those who will be resurrected and those who will be returned to earth, body and soul, from Heaven. The bodies of the resurrected will already be on earth in some form and will be joined with their spirits, which are now in Heaven.

Those who will be returned to earth, body and soul, from Heaven are Enoch[173] and Elijah[174], who had been raptured in Old Testament times, and the two witnesses[175], who will have been raptured in mid-Tribulation.

3. Those Resurrected During the 75-Day Interval
a. The Old Testament Saints

All Old Testament Jewish and Gentile saints from the days of Adam to Pentecost will be resurrected during the 75-day interval period to dwell on earth during the Kingdom.

---

[172] Daniel 12:5-13
[173] Genesis 5:24; Hebrews 11:5
[174] 2nd Kings 2:11
[175] Revelation chapter 11

1) The Old Testament Israelite Saints

Matthew 24:31: He will send out his angels with a loud trumpet, and they will gather his elect from the four winds, from one end of the sky to the other.

Mark 13:27: gather his elect from the four winds, from the ends of the earth to the ends of heaven.

The Biblical context indicates that *His elect* refers to Israelite saints. The Lord will send forth His angels to gather the bodies of deceased Israelites from the *earth* to join their spirits gathered from *Heaven*.
Daniel 12:1-2 provides the timing:

> At that time
> Michael, the great prince who stands
> watch over your people, will rise up.
>
> There will be a time of distress such as
> never has occurred since nations came
> into being until that time.
>
> But at that time all your people who are
> found written in the book will escape.
>
> Many who sleep in the dust of the earth
> will awake, some to eternal life, and
> some to disgrace and eternal contempt.
> ~ Daniel 12:1-2 ~

Millennial Kingdom of God on Planet Earth

Your people, Daniel's people, are the Jews.
After the *time of distress*, the Tribulation, those deceased Israelites worthy of *everlasting life* will be resurrected to dwell in the Kingdom.

Those unworthy will be resurrected at the very end of the Millennium to face the Great White Throne Judgment (Revelation 20:11).

2) Old Testament Gentile Saints

Matthew 8:5-12: Jesus & the Centurion
> ...the centurion said, "Lord, I am not worthy for You to come under my roof, but just say the word, and my servant will be healed. ... Now when Jesus heard this, He marveled a and said ...
> "Truly I say to you, I have not found such great faith with anyone in Israel.
> "I say to you that many will come from east a and west, and recline at the table with Abraham, Isaac and Jacob in the kingdom ... but the sons of the kingdom will be cast out into the outer darkness; in that place there will be weeping ...
> ~ Matthew 8:5-12 ~

That the centurion was a Gentile is clear from Matthew 8:10 and by the fact that Jesus contrasted him with *the sons of the kingdom*, that people to whom the promises of the Kingdom were made, the Jews.

That the centurion and other believing Gentiles will have a place in the Kingdom is made plain by verse 11 and by the fact that Jesus identified him as a case in point.

That he was an Old Testament believer when he exercised faith is clear by the fact that he did so before the cross; and, of course, he, as well as all other Old Testament Gentile believers, would need to be resurrected and gathered *from east and west, to recline at the table with Abraham, Isaac and Jacob in the kingdom.*

Since
> *flesh and blood cannot inherit the kingdom of God; nor can corruption inherit incorruption*[176],

and the Biblical text does not record resurrection of Old Testament Gentile Saints after the Millennium Kingdom begins or during the prior 7-year Tribulation, it may well be that they will be resurrected during the 75-day Interval period about the same time as the resurrection of the Old Testament Israelite saints.

b. The Martyred Tribulation Saints

Multitudes of those who exercise faith in Messiah during the Tribulation will be slain (Revelation 7:7-11); but Revelation 20:4 says of them, *and they came to*

---
[176] 1st Corinthians 15:50

life and reigned with Christ for a thousand years.

Since they are to reign with Christ *for a thousand years*, they will need to be resurrected before the thousand-year Kingdom begins.

4. Those Born into the Kingdom

Some people enter the Kingdom with glorified bodies, and some with natural bodies; and according to Matthew 22:28-30, no one with a glorified body will bear children:

For in the resurrection they neither marry nor are given in marriage, but are like angels in heaven.

However, those who enter the kingdom with natural bodies will bear children who, like their parents, will have natural bodies; and they too will bear children.

B. Will Angels Dwell on Earth in the Kingdom?

Angels will return to earth with Jesus and the body of Christ (Matthew 25:31), an angel will bind Satan in the abyss for the duration of the Millennium (Revelation 20:1-3) and angels will gather all Old Testament Jewish believers to the Promised land (Daniel 12:1-2; Matthew 24:31; Mark 13:27); but Scripture simply does not say whether Angels will dwell on Earth during the Millennial Kingdom.

C. Animals and Plants
Such passages as Isaiah 65:25 and Micah 4:4 show that there will be animals and plants in the Kingdom:
> Isaiah 65:25: The wolf and the lamb will graze together, and the lion will eat straw like the ox; and dust will be the serpent's food.

> Micah 4:4: Each of them will sit under his vine and under his fig tree, with no one to make them afraid, for the mouth of the LORD of hosts has spoken.

During the Millennial Kingdom the behavior of animals will be changed. Animals will not devour or harm one another or harm even a little child[177].

BODILY NATURE OF KINGDOM INHABITANTS[178]
Saved Mortals Surviving the Tribulation
Those saved mortals alive on earth at the end of the Tribulation will remain on earth through the transitional period and the commencement of the Kingdom and will retain their natural, mortal bodies. The fact that there will be death in the Millennial Kingdom corroborates this.[179]

This group includes the Israelites saved during the Tribulation and the sheep Gentiles.

---
[177] See Isaiah 11:8
[178] Adapted from Norman Manzon, *The Inhabitants of the Kingdom*
[179] See Isaiah 65:17-25; 1st Corinthians 15:20-26

Those Who Return from Heaven

Those raised bodily to Heaven and returned to earth will have glorified bodies[180] including Enoch, Elijah and the two witnesses who will return from Heaven.

Those Resurrected During the 75-day Interval

All the righteous who will be resurrected during the transitional period will have glorified bodies.[181]

Daniel 12:1-2 refers specifically to the bodies of the deceased faithful in Daniel's day and indicates that their spirits will experience eternal life, and their bodies will awaken *to everlasting life*. This indicates resurrection in glorified bodies because if these saints will arise in their natural bodies, which would die again, it could not be said that their bodies will awaken *to everlasting life*.

THOSE WHO WILL NOT ENTER THE KINGDOM

While a man or woman cannot *earn* entrance into God's Kingdom - that is a gift that God must bestow[182] - it is plain from Scripture that willful rebellion against God's standard of righteousness will keep a man out of the Kingdom:

> Now the works of the flesh are obvious: sexual immorality, moral impurity,

---

[180] See 1st Corinthians 15:50-54
[181] 1st Corinthians 15:50-54
[182] Ephesians 2:8. See Habakkuk 2:4

promiscuity, idolatry, sorcery, hatreds, strife, jealousy, outbursts of anger, selfish ambitions, envy, drunkenness, carousing, and anything similar.
I am warning you about these things—as I warned you before—that those who practice such things will not inherit the kingdom of God.[183]

---

[183] Galatians 5:19-21; Matthew 7:13-14, 21-23

Millennial Kingdom of God on Planet Earth

Chapter 10
Duration of the Millennial Kingdom

Biblical Truth: When Jesus returns to Earth he will establish his Messianic Millennial Kingdom of God, the Son for **1,000 years**:
> Then I saw thrones, and the people sitting on them had been given the authority to judge. And I saw the souls of those who had been beheaded for their testimony about Jesus and for proclaiming the word of God. They had not worshiped the beast or his statue, nor accepted his mark on their foreheads or their hands. They all came to life again, and they reigned with Christ for a **thousand years.**
> [WORD of GOD in Revelation 20:4 New Living Translation]

WORD OF GOD VERSUS THE WORD OF MANKIND
The Disciples believed that at Jesus' Second Coming he would establish his Messianic Millennial Kingdom of God, the Son for 1,000 years.
The Church of Jesus Christ at Pentecost believed that.

The Revelation of the resurrected Jesus Christ made known to the Apostle John, recorded

> not only once,[184]
> not only twice,[185]
> not only three times,[186]
> not only four times.[187]
> not only five times,[188]
> but SIX times[189]

that Jesus' coming Kingdom on Planet Earth would last 1,000 years.

And, no verse of Scripture specifically states that Jesus' coming Kingdom on Planet Earth would not last 1,000 years.

The current author believes that all Scripture is inspired by the LORD God Almighty[190] and that the LORD God, through his Holy Spirit, has the ability to say what he means and to mean what he says.

The word of Mankind

Jesus Christ was a Jew; all the original disciples were Jews; the first generation of Christian leaders was Jewish, centered in Jerusalem.

---

[184] Revelation 20:2
[185] Revelation 20:3
[186] Revelation 20:4
[187] Revelation 20:5
[188] Revelation 20:6
[189] Revelation 20:7
[190] 2nd Timothy 3"16

But, the expanding church soon contained more Gentiles than Jews. In addition, the character of Jewish led Jerusalem changed when Rome destroyed the Jewish Temple in 70A.D. and the Jews, including Jewish Christians, were forced to flee.

Thereafter, the church's new leadership were Gentiles coming from other Christian centers in Antioch and, eventually, Rome - both Gentile cities.

In an attempt to define themselves as the true inheritors of Israel's relationship with God, Gentile church leaders espoused a theory of Replacement Theology claiming the Institutional church had replaced the Jewish people in God's program and that the only thing the Jewish nation could look forward to was condemnation.

The antagonism of the early Christians towards the Jews was reflected in the writings of the early Church Fathers. Justin Martyr was the first, about 160 A.D. to espouse the theory that the Christian church was the true spiritual Israel. For example, Justin Martyr (in speaking to a Jew is alleged to have said:
  "The Scriptures are not yours, but ours."[191]

---

[191] Citation attributed to Justin Martyr by Clarence H. Wagner, Jr, in *The Error of Replacement Theology*, p.1, *http://www.ldolphin.org/replacement/* (accessed 12/02/20). Also attributed to Irenaeus by Jim Showers in *Replacement Theology: The Black Sheep of Christendom Part Two*, p.2, Israel My Glory, May/June 2010.

Justin's views laid the groundwork for the growing belief that the church had superseded or replaced Israel.[192]

Irenaeus, writing around 181A.D. said,
> **They who boast themselves, being the house of Jacob and the people of Israel, are disinherited from the grace of God."[193]**

And, after all the original disciples had died, and more than 200 years after Jesus' crucifixion, Origen, the most prolific writer of the early church, grounded his Replacement Theology in allegorical interpretation. Origen when explaining that Jesus was sent to the "lost sheep of the **house of Israel"[194] argued that the lost sheep are not Jews, who are "carnal" Israel, but Christians, who are "heavenly" Israel. [195]**

The replacement concept gained additional long-lasting effect with Aurelius Augustine of Hippo, a North African church father in the 5th century A.D., who furthered Justin Martyr's idea that the church was the new [*Spiritual*] Israel. Augustine was strongly

---

[192] Justin Martyr, *Dialogue with Trypho* 11:1-5
[193] **Irenaeus, "Against Heresies," The Anti-Nicene Fathers, ed. A. Roberts and J. Donaldson, vol. 1 (1885; reprint, Grand Rapids: Eerdmans, 1993), 3.21.1**
[194] Matthew 15:24
[195] Origen, "De Principiis," The Anti-Nicene Fathers, ed. A. Roberts and J. Donaldson, vol. 4 (1885; reprint, Grand Rapids: Eerdmans, 1994), 4.1.22.

influenced by both Ambrose of Milan, a church leader who argued that the Jewish people were irrevocably perverse and not worthy of any good thought, and Origen's use of allegory to interpret Scripture.

Augustine used allegory to formulate the system we today call Amillennialism[196] which popularized Justin Martyr's view that the Christian church was the true "spiritual" Israel and fostered the view that there is no future kingdom for Israel and no 1,000-year earthly Millennial Kingdom period despite the clear words of Scripture to that effect repeated six (6) times in the first seven verses of Revelation, Chapter 20.

Amillennialism denies a future earthly Kingdom for Faithful Followers of Jesus, including Believing ethnic

---

[196] The word, millennium, means one thousand years.
It is a combination of two Latin words mille (thousand) and annum (year). Amillennial, literally means "no one thousand years" because in the Greek language one of the ways of negating something is to put the letter "a" in front of it.
    We do the same in English using the prefix "un".
    For example, to negate the term "ethical" we say "unethical."

Amillennialism is the belief that there is no literal 1000-year physical reign of Jesus from Jerusalem on Planet Earth. Thus, adherents of this view regard the 1,000 years clearly spelled out six times in chapter 20 of Revelation, as merely a symbolic number, not a literal period of time.
Amillennialists also generally believe that Israel has been permanently set aside for all time and that God's current Kingdom plan involves only the Church.
Jim Showers, *Replacement Theology: The Black Sheep of Christendom Part Two*, Israel My Glory, May/June 2010

Millennial Kingdom of God on Planet Earth

Jews, in which Christ reigns on earth for a thousand years and fulfills all the Old Covenant promises.

In amillennialists' view the church replaces Israel and the blessings are spiritual. In their view, the Kingdom of God then becomes only a spiritual Kingdom and a heavenly Kingdom and not an earthly kingdom at all.[197]

Despite his brilliance, Augustine failed to use proper exegesis in his teaching concerning the Biblical account of the End-Times.
Augustine, who was a vegetarian and as a Bishop had become increasingly ascetic, recorded that he once believed, as the Bible teaches[198], that Christ would, after his Second Coming, establish an 1,000-year (millennial) kingdom on Planet Earth.[199]

But. not by God-voiced[200] Biblical texts but because of the words of false teachers of his day, Augustine decided that the WORD of God concerning an earthly 1,000-year (millennial) kingdom was not to be believed because those false teachers taught that the millennium

---

[197] See The Lutheran Church-Missouri Synod; https://www.lcms.org/belief-and-practice; Dr. John MacArthur, Sermon, *Why Every Calvinist Should Be a Premillennialist*, Part 3, (2007) available at http://m.gty.org/Resources/Sermons/90-336

[198] Revelation 20:1-7
[199] Augustine, *City of God*, Book XX, chapter 7
[200] 2nd Timothy 3:16

was to be as a thousand years of reveling in "carnal" and "immoderate" pleasures.[201]

Augustine wrote:

> those who then rise again shall enjoy the leisure of immoderate carnal banquets, furnished with an amount of meat and drink such as not only to shock the feeling of the temperate, but even to surpass the measure of credulity itself, such assertions can be believed only by the carnal.[202]

Then, instead of validating his new opinion from the WORD of God, Augustine avoided proper exegesis[203] and substituted eisegesis[204] by simply declaring:

> It were a **tedious process to refute** these opinions point by point: we prefer proceeding to show how that passage of Scripture should be understood.[205]

Then Augustine proceeded to use a theological presupposition rather than an exegesis of the text and opined that End-Times Scripture involved a broader

---

[201] Frank A. James III., *Augustine's Millennial Views*, *Christian History*, Issue 15 (1987)

[202] Augustine, *City of God*, Book XX, chapter 7 [emphasis added]

[203] Exegesis is the process of careful, analytical study of biblical passages to produce useful interpretations of those passages. Ideally, exegesis involves the analysis of the biblical text in the language of its original or earliest available form.

[204] Eisegesis is the opposite of exegesis (to draw out). Eisegesis means (to draw in). An eisegetic commentator "imports" or "draws in" substituting into the text his or her own purely subjective interpretations which are unsupported by the text itself.

[205] *Ibid.*

Millennial Kingdom of God on Planet Earth

view of the thousand years, as a term marking an indefinite period of time between Jesus' first coming when Christ's kingdom was established, and Jesus' future second advent.

During this span of time, writes Augustine, the devil is "prevented from the exercise of his whole power to seduce men" and the saints "reign with Christ" over his spiritual kingdom. *[ed. is Satan active today or not?]*

And then, when Christ returns, he will judge the living and the dead, and thereafter usher in the eternal state.[206]

Augustine's conclusions were very influential.
The Catholic Church during the Medieval period built its system of eschatology on Augustinian amillennialism, where Christ rules the earth **spiritually** through his triumphant church.
During the Reformation theologians such as John Calvin accepted amillennialism.[207]

Augustine's views enhanced and solidified the power, prestige and prominence of the Institutional church throughout the Middle Ages and his spiritual view of

---

[206] Frank A. James III., *Augustine's Millennial Views*, *Christian History*, Issue 15 (1987)
[207] *Blomberg, Craig L. (2006). From Pentecost to Patmos: An Introduction to Acts Through Revelation, p.519*

the millennial kingdom became the predominant view of the traditional church.

With some variations, amillennialism remains as the traditional eschatology of the Anglican, Roman Catholic, Calvinist (Presbyterian, Reformed), Eastern Orthodox, Lutheran and Methodist Churches.[208]

AUTHOR'S CONCLUSION AS TO THE DURATION OF THE MILLENNIAL KINGDOM

We should not allow differences in our viewpoints on the Millennium to divide us. It has been well said:
> In essentials, unity
> in non-essentials, liberty
> in all things, charity.[209]

Yet, the fact remains that the true test is what does the Bible say with the context determining the meaning.

Tradition and what other humans may have believed down through church history is really not the issue unless it is grounded in Scripture.

Accordingly. after weighing all the evidence, this Compiler concludes:

---

[208] *Jon Kennedy, The Everything Jesus Book: His Life, His Teachings. Adams Media. (2006).*

[209] Philipp Melanchthon [Martin Luther's advisor in the Reformation].

Millennial Kingdom of God on Planet Earth

The Biblical Text best clearly states and supports the understanding that Jesus of Nazareth, the Messiah, will return bodily to planet Earth before He reigns here for a thousand years with His saints.

I saw an angel coming down out of heaven, having the key of the abyss and a great chain in his hand. He seized the dragon, the old serpent, which is the devil and Satan, who deceives the whole inhabited earth, and bound him for a thousand years, and cast him into the abyss, and shut it, and sealed it over him that he should deceive the nations no more, until the thousand years were finished. After this, he must be freed for a short time.

I saw thrones, and they sat on them, and judgment was given to them. I saw the souls of those who had been beheaded for the testimony of Jesus, and for the word of God, and such as didn't worship the beast nor his image, and didn't receive the mark on their forehead and on their hand. They lived and reigned with Christ for a thousand years.
The rest of the dead didn't live until the thousand years were finished. This is the first resurrection.

Blessed and holy is he who has part in the first resurrection. Over these, the second death has no power, but they will be priests of God and of Christ, and will reign with him one thousand years.

And after the thousand years, Satan will be released from his prison, and he will come out to deceive the nations which are in the four corners of the earth, Gog and Magog, to gather them together to the war... [WORD of GOD in Rev. 20:1-8]

The question remains:
> will there be an actual 1,000-year Kingdom reign of Jesus from Jerusalem on Planet Earth as the Biblical text says or just a spiritual rule for an indefinite time period as the Amillennialists insist?
>
> The answer is that your or my personal opinion will not be determinative. At his Second Coming the LORD will establish the duration of his Messianic Kingdom according to his will so that
>> at the name of Jesus
>> every knee will bow—
>> in heaven and on earth
>> and under the earth—
>> and every tongue will confess
>> that Jesus Christ is Lord,
>> to the glory of God the Father.[210]

---

[210] Philippians 2:10-11

Millennial Kingdom of God on Planet Earth

Chapter 11
Quality of Life in Jesus' Kingdom

PHYSICAL CHARACTERISTICS

1. Topography and geography of the earth changed[211]
2. Wild animals will be tamed[212]
3. Crops will be abundant[213]
4. Human longevity will be increased[214]

SPIRITUAL/RELIGIOUS CHARACTERISTICS- EVENTS

1. Satan will be confined in the abyss[215]
2. Millennial temple will be built [216]
3. Sacrifices offered as memorials to Christ's death[217]
4. Feasts of the New Year, Passover, and Tabernacles will be reinstituted[218]
5. Nations will worship in Jerusalem[219]
6. Worldwide knowledge of God[220]
7. Holy Spirit fills and empowers Israel[221]

---

[211] Adapted from https://www.preceptaustin.org/the_millennium 3
Isaiah 2:2; Ezekiel 47:1-12; Ezekiel 48:8-20; Zechariah 14:4, 8, 10
[212] Isaiah 11:6-9; Isaiah 35:9; Ezekiel 34:25
[213] Isaiah 27:6; 35:1-2, 6-7; Amos 9:13; Zechariah 14:8
[214] Isaiah 65:20-23
[215] Revelation 20:1-3
[216] Ezekiel 40:5-43:27
[217] Isaiah 56:7; 66:20-23; Jeremiah 33:17-18; Ezekiel 43:18-27; Ezekiel 45:13-46:24; Malachi 3:3-4
[218] Ezekiel 45:18-25; Zechariah 14:16-21
[219] Isaiah 2:2-4; Micah 4:2, 7:12; Zechariah 8:20-23, 14:16-21
[220] Isaiah 11:9; Jeremiah 31:34; Micah 4:5; Habakkuk 2:14; Zechariah 14:9; Revelation 11:15; Revelation 15:4
[221] Isaiah 32:15; 44:3; Ezekiel 36:24-29, 39:29; Joel 2:28-29

Millennial Kingdom of God on Planet Earth

8. New Covenant with Israel will be fulfilled[222]
9. Righteousness and justice will prevail[223]

POLITICAL CHARACTERISTICS AND EVENTS

1. Israel will be reunited as a nation[224]
2. Israel will be at peace in the land[225]
3. Israel's Abrahamic Covenant land-grant boundaries will be established[226]
4. Jesus Christ will rule over Israel from Jerusalem[227]
5. Davidic Covenant will be fulfilled with Christ on the throne of David in Jerusalem[228]
6. Jesus Christ will rule over and judge the nations[229]
7. Resurrected saints will reign with Jesus[230]
8. Universal peace will prevail[231]
9. Jerusalem will become the world's capital[232]
10. The world will be blessed through Israel[233]

---

[222] Jeremiah 31:31-34; Ezekiel 11:19-20, 36:25-32
[223] Isaiah 9:7; Isaiah 11:4, 42:1-4; Jeremiah 23:5
[224] Jeremiah 3:18; Ezekiel 37:15-23. Occurred May 14, 1948.
[225] Deuteronomy 30:1-10; Isaiah 32:18; Hosea 14:5, 7; Amos 9:15; Micah 4:4, Micah 5:4-5; Zechariah 3:10, 14:11
[226] Genesis 15:18-21; Ezekiel 47:13-48:8, 23-27
[227] Micah 4:7, 5:2; see Isaiah 40:11
[228] 2nd Samuel 7:11-16; Isaiah 9:6-7; Jeremiah 33:17-26; Amos 9:11-12; Luke 1:32-33
[229] Isaiah 11:3-5; Micah 4:2-3; Zechariah 14:9; Revelation 19:15
[230] Matthew 19:28; 2nd Timothy 2:12; Rev\elation 5:10, 20:4
[231] Isaiah 2:4, 32:17-18, 60:18; Hosea 2:18; Micah 4:2-4, 5:4; Zechariah 9:10
[232] Jeremiah 3:17; Ezekiel 48:30-35; Joel 3:16-17; Micah 4:1, 6-8; Zechariah 8:2-3
[233] Genesis 12:1-3, 22:18, 26:3-4, 28:13-14

OUR ROLE DURING THE MILLENNIAL KINGDOM

What's going to happen to us during this Messianic Kingdom of Christ?   Many things.

One of the things that's going to happen is you, as a resurrected person at the rapture, returning with Jesus Christ at the end of the tribulation period, are going to be ruling and reigning with Jesus Christ under His delegated authority.

Revelation 5:10 indicates this when it says, "You have made them to be a kingdom of priests and to our God and they will reign upon the **earth**."
That's your destiny as a Christian.

There's a heavenly program to be sure for seven years during the Tribulation but that's not where the bulk of our time is spent; it's ruling and reigning with Christ on the earth. Not because He needs us but because He wants to use us under delegated authority.[234]
Daniel 9:27 spells it out very clearly:
> The kingdom, dominion, and greatness
> of the kingdoms under all of heaven will be
> given to the people, the holy ones of the Most
> High. His kingdom will be an everlasting
> kingdom, and all rulers will serve and obey Him.

---

[234] Dr. Andy Woods, *Daniel*, retrieved at http://www.spiritandtruth.org/teaching/Daniel_by_Andy_Woods/26_Daniel_7_26-28/20170618_26_daniel_7_26-28_transcript.html?x=x

Millennial Kingdom of God on Planet Earth

I believe that what Daniel is speaking of here is the Millennial Kingdom, the thousand-year reign of Jesus of Nazareth, the Messiah, a specific time-period clearly delineated six times in Revelation 20:1-8:

> I saw an angel coming down out of heaven, having the key of the abyss and a great chain in his hand.
> He seized the dragon, the old serpent, which is the devil and Satan, who deceives the whole inhabited earth, and bound him for a **thousand years**, and cast him into the abyss, and shut it, and sealed it over him, that he should deceive the nations no more, until the **thousand years** were finished. After this, he must be freed for a short time.
> I saw thrones, and they sat on them, and judgment was given to them.
> I saw the souls of those who had been beheaded for the testimony of Jesus, and for the word of God, and such as didn't worship the beast nor his image, and didn't receive the mark on their forehead and on their hand. They lived and reigned with Christ for a **thousand years**.
>> The rest of the dead didn't live until the **thousand years** were finished. This is the first resurrection.
>> Blessed and holy is he who has part in the first resurrection. Over these, the second death

has no power, but they will be **priests** of God and of Christ and will reign with him **one thousand years**.

And after the **thousand years**, Satan will be released from his prison, and he will come out to deceive the nations...
[WORD of God in Revelation 20:1-8 WEB emphasis added]

Titus 2:13 refers to this period as our Blessed Hope: looking for the blessed hope and appearing of the glory of our great God and Savior, Jesus Christ

And Revelation 11:15 points to this as the culmination of God's eternal plan:
The seventh angel sounded *[his trumpet]*, and great voices in heaven followed, saying, "The kingdom of the world has become the Kingdom of our Lord, and of his Christ. He will reign forever and ever!" [WEB]

Accordingly, what the Lord is doing right now in our lives is training and preparing us, you and me, for the kingdom rule and authority that we will wield in this coming kingdom.[235]

---

[235] *Ibid.*

Millennial Kingdom of God on Planet Earth

God has chosen the humble, not the proud. He has chosen the poor, not the rich. He has chosen the weak, not the noble or strong. He has chosen a select group of people of this earth that you would not consider leaders in this life, but by the Holy Spirit, God calls them.[236]

---

[236] **1st Corinthians 1:25-29**

Chapter 12
Government of the Millennial Kingdom of Jesus

The Messianic Millennial Kingdom of Jesus of Nazareth, the Messiah, will be administered through an absolute monarchy with a definite chain of command and lines of delegated authority.

The delegated authority will be split into two branches:
    a Gentile Branch of government and
    a Jewish Branch of government.

It will look like this:

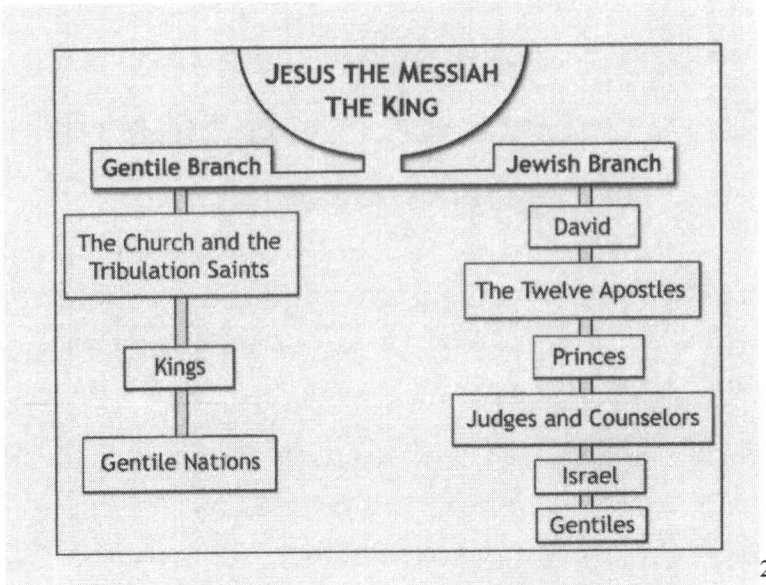

Millennial Kingdom of God on Planet Earth

```
                    JESUS THE MESSIAH
                        THE KING
    ┌─ Gentile Branch ─┐      ┌─ Jewish Branch ─┐
                                    David
    The Church and the
    Tribulation Saints          The Twelve Apostles
          Kings                      Princes
                                Judges and Counselors
      Gentile Nations                 Israel
                                     Gentiles
```
237

POLITICAL CHARACTERISTICS OF CHRIST'S MILLENNIAL REIGN[238]

THE BIBLICAL FACTS: When the Messianic Millennial Kingdom begins all natural men, both Gentiles and Jews will be believers in Jesus, the Messiah.[239]

---

[237] Chart from Dr. Arnold Fruchtenbaum, Footsteps of the Messiah. P.387
[238] Adapted from Dr. David Reagan, *The Millennium in the Old Testament*, p.1 retrieved at http://christinprophecy.org/articles/the-millennium-in-the-old-testament/.
[239] Dr. Peter John Moses, *Israel and the Church*, p. 11.

The Remnant of Israel will have been redeemed.[240]

Regeneration is the work of the Holy Spirit, and the nation of Israel will be regenerated because of the outpouring of the Holy Spirit on them, accompanied by wonders in the heavens, resulting in the deliverance and escape of the living Remnant of the Jewish population.[241]

The Remnant of Israel will have been restored.[242]

Israel will be reunited as a nation.[243]

The reign of Jesus Christ will be world-wide, [244] **as Christ rules over and judges the nations.**[245]

Jesus' throne will be established in Jerusalem.[246]

---

[240] Zechariah 12:10; Matthew 23-37-39. See Isaiah 12:1-2; Leviticus 26:39-42; Jeremiah 3:12-18; Hosea 5:15-6:3
[241] Joel 2:28-32; Dr. Arnold Fruchtenbaum, *Campaigns of Armageddon,* p.20. Retrieved from https://www.raptureready.com/rr-armageddon.html
[242] Zephaniah 3:18-20
[243] Jeremiah 3:18; Ezekiel 37:15-23. May 14, 1948.
[244] Isaiah 2:2, 9:6-7; Zechariah 14:9
[245] Isaiah 11:1-5; Micah 4:2-3; Zechariah 14:9
[246] Micah 4:1-7; Zechariah 8:3

Millennial Kingdom of God on Planet Earth

Jesus will fulfill the Davidic Covenant by ruling on the throne of David in Jerusalem.[247]

Jerusalem will become the world's capital.[248] **Because the Lord will be reigning from Jerusalem, the nation of Israel will be the prime nation in the world.**[249]

The Government of the Millennial Kingdom will be a theocratic one with Jesus serving as king, legislator and judge.[250]

The resurrected saints will reign with Christ.[251]

Justice will prevail.[252]

Peace will prevail.[253]

Israel will be at peace in its land.[254]

---

[247] Luke 1:32-33; Isaiah 2:2-4, 9:7, 24:23; 2nd Samuel 7:11-16; 1st Chronicles 17:11–14; 2nd Chronicles 6:16; Jeremiah 33:15-26; Micah 4:7; Psalm 2:6, 110:2, 132:11-18; Amos 9:11-12; Zechariah 2:10-11, 6:12-13, 14:9. See Isaiah 16:5.
[248] Jeremiah 3:17; Micah 4:1-8; see Zechariah 8:2-3
[249] Isaiah 2:2-3, 49:22-23, 60:1-62:7]
[250] Isaiah 33:17-22
[251] Matthew 19:28; 2nd Timothy 2:12; Revelation 5:10, 20:4,,6
[World English Bible]
[252] Isaiah 1:26-27, 9:7, 11:5, 32:16, 42:1-4; Jeremiah 23:5; see Isaiah 65:21-23
[253] Isaiah 2:4, 32:17-18, 60:18; Hosea 2:18; Micah 4:3; Zechariah 9:10
[254] Isaiah 32:18, 60:18; Ezekiel 28:26; Micah 4:1-7; 5:4; Zechariah 14:11

There will be freedom from oppression.[255]

The Abrahamic Covenant land-grant boundaries of Israel will be established.[256]

The world will be blessed through Israel.[257]

JEWISH BRANCH OF GOVERNMENT

The absolute monarchy of Jesus of Nazareth, the Messiah will extend to Israel and the Gentile nations.

Jesus promised his Disciples that in the Messianic Age, when he [Jesus] sits on His glorious throne on Earth, the Disciples who followed him will also sit on 12 thrones, judging the 12 tribes of Israel. [258]
[WORD of GOD in Matthew 19:28]

---

[255] Isaiah. 14:3-6
[256] Genesis 15:18-21; Ezekiel 47:13-48:8, 23-27
[257] Genesis 12:3; 28:14. See Acts 3:25; Galatians 3:8; Micah 4:1-8; Zechariah 8:20-23, 14:16
[258] For detailed discussion of the Jewish Branch of Government see Dr. Arnold Fruchtenbaum, *Footsteps of the Messiah*, p.396

Millennial Kingdom of God on Planet Earth

Gentile [Church] Branch of Government

The roll of the Believing Church in Jesus' Messianic Millennial Kingdom is detailed in Revelation 20:4-6. The Believing Church and the Tribulation Saints will co-reign over the Gentile nations and carry out Jesus' decrees to those nations.

> Then I saw thrones, and people seated on them who were given authority to judge. I also saw the souls of those who had been beheaded because of their testimony about Jesus and because of the word of God, who had not worshiped the beast or his image, and who had not accepted the mark on their foreheads or their hands. They came to life and reigned with Christ for a **thousand years**. The rest of the dead did not come to life until the **thousand years** were completed.
>
> This is the first resurrection. Blessed and holy is the one who shares in the first resurrection! The second death has no power over them, but they will be priests of God and of Christ, and they will reign with him for a **thousand years**.
> [WORD of GOD in Rev. 20:4-6, emphasis added]

WHAT ARE THE LAWS OF THE KINGDOM?[259]

A kingdom - like any nation today - cannot function without laws. There must be a standard of conduct for subjects and citizens to follow, or chaos and anarchy would result. Merely following the laws of a kingdom or nation does not grant a person citizenship.

Laws are enacted for people to follow to ensure cohesion, agreement, and peace in civil and interpersonal relationships. Without an understood standard, enforced by a sovereign ruler, everyone would act according to his own whim or desire, sometimes to the detriment of others. [Judges 21:25].

The Lord is not the author of confusion or disorder.[260] His Kingdom will be peaceful and orderly because everyone who initially enters into it will have voluntarily submitted themselves to the law - the commandments- of God. Jesus will not have anyone in His Kingdom who demonstrates, by the pattern of his life, that he will not obey Him.[261]

Revelation 12:17 describes the Israeli Remnant as those "who keep the commandments of God and hold firmly to the testimony of Jesus Christ."

---

[259] Adapted from http: www.truegospel.org/index.cfm/fuseaction/basics.tour/ID/6/What-are-Laws-of-Kingdom.htm
[260] 1st Corinthians 14:33
[261] Matthew 7:21-23; Hebrews 10:16-17, 26-31

Millennial Kingdom of God on Planet Earth

A Pharisee once asked Jesus, "Teacher, which is the greatest commandment in the law?"[262] Jesus' response shows that the intent behind God's law is *love* - love toward God, and love toward fellow man:

Jesus said to him,
> "Love the Lord your God with all your heart, with all your soul, and with all your mind. This is the greatest and most important command.
> The second is like it: Love your neighbor as yourself.
> All the Law and the Prophets depend on these two commands."
> [WORD of GOD in Matthew 22:37-40]

These two statements - loving God and loving neighbor as oneself - encapsulate the first four and the last six commandments respectively.

The commandments further define *how* to love God and love mankind.

We love God in general by placing Him first, by not adopting physical aids in worshipping Him, by not bearing His name in vain, and by keeping the seventh-day Sabbath holy.

---

[262] Matthew 22:38

We love mankind, in general, by honoring our parents, not murdering, not committing adultery, not stealing, not lying, and not coveting.

At Jesus' First Coming he revealed the spirit - the *intent* - of His law.

He showed that the sixth commandment extends much further than merely prohibiting the taking of human life, but covers even hating.[263] Similarly, the intent behind the seventh commandment is to stop adultery at its source: the heart.[264]

Following God's commandments in both their letter and spirit ensures the best quality of life for everyone.

When Jesus was asked what one must do to have eternal life, His response was simple: "If you want to enter into [eternal] life, *keep the commandments*".[265]

To reinforce this, at the conclusion of the Last Supper before His arrest and crucifixion, Jesus instructed his disciples:

If you love me, you will keep my commands.[266]

> The one who has my commands and keeps them is the one who loves me. And the one who loves me will be loved by my Father.

---

[263] Matthew 5:21-22
[264] Matthew 5:27-28
[265] Matthew 19:16-17
[266] John 14:15

> I also will love him and will reveal myself to him.[267]

> If anyone loves me, he will keep my word. My Father will love him, and we will come to him and make our home with him. The one who doesn't love me will not keep my words. The word that you hear is not mine but is **from the Father** who sent me.[268]

The apostle James called the Ten Commandments "the Royal Law" - meaning that it came from a King, and is worthy of his Kingdom:

> Indeed, if you fulfill the **royal law** prescribed in the Scripture, Love your neighbor as yourself, you are doing well. If, however, you show favoritism, you commit sin and are convicted by the law as transgressors. For whoever keeps the entire law, and yet stumbles at one point, is guilty of breaking it all.
> For he who said, Do not commit adultery, also said Do not murder.
> So if you do not commit adultery, but you murder, you are a lawbreaker. Speak and act as those who are to be judged by the law of freedom.[269]

---

[267] John 14:21
[268] John 14:23-24 [emphasis added]
[269] James 2:8-2 [emphasis added]

Chapter 13

Worship in the Messianic Kingdom

BIBLICAL TRUTHS:

I have come to gather all nations and
languages; they will come and see my glory...
And they will proclaim my glory among the
nations.
From one month to the next and from
one week to the next all people will come
to worship me," declares J^{e}hovah.
   [WORD of GOD in Isaiah 66:18-19, 23]

so that at the name of Jesus
every knee will bow—
in heaven and on earth
and under the earth—
and every tongue will confess
that Jesus Christ is Lord,
to the glory of God the Father.
   [WORD of GOD in Philippians 2:10-11]

Millennial Kingdom of God on Planet Earth

Worship during the Messianic Millennial Kingdom will focus on worship to and adoration of God, the Father and God, the Son Jesus Christ.[270]

Perhaps akin to:
> **Praise our God,**
> **all his servants, and the ones who fear him,**
> **both small and great!**
> > **Hallelujah, because our Lord God, the Almighty, and Jesus, the Messiah reign!**[271]

A new Temple will be built in Jerusalem for use during the Millennium.

Worship during the Messianic Millennial Kingdom will center around that temple.

The Millennial Temple

Numerous passages of Scripture indicate that there will be a physical Temple in Jerusalem during the Millennial Kingdom on earth:
> Isaiah 2:1-3 [emphasis added]:
> > the vision that Isaiah … saw concerning Judah and Jerusalem:

---

[270] Isaiah 12:1-6; 25:1-26:19; 56:7; 61:10-11; 66:23; Jeremiah 33:11, 18, 21-22; Ezekiel 20:40-41; 40:1-46:24; Zechariah 6:12-15; 8:20-23; 14:16-21
[271] See Revelation 19:5-6

In the last days
the mountain of the **Lord's house** will be
established at the top of the mountains and
will be raised above the hills.
All nations will stream to it, and many peoples
will come and say,
"Come, let's go up to the mountain of the Lord,
to the **house of the God of Jacob**.
He will teach us about his ways
so that we may walk in his paths."
For instruction will go out of Zion and the
word of the Lord from Jerusalem.

Isaiah 56:1, 6-8 [emphasis added]:
    Preserve justice and do what is right,
    for my salvation is coming soon,
    and my righteousness will be revealed. …
As for the foreigners who join themselves to the Lord
to minister to him, to love the name of the Lord,
and to become his servants—
all who keep the Sabbath without desecrating it
and who hold firmly to my covenant—
    I will bring them to **my holy mountain**
    and let them rejoice in **my house of prayer**.
    Their burnt offerings and sacrifices
    will be acceptable on my altar,
    for my house will be called a house of prayer
    for all nations.

Millennial Kingdom of God on Planet Earth

> This is the declaration of the Lord God,
> who gathers the dispersed of Israel:

Isaiah 60:13-15, 18 [emphasis added]:
> The glory of Lebanon will come to you—
> its pine, elm, and cypress together—
> to beautify the place of **my sanctuary**,
> and I will glorify **my dwelling place**.
> The sons of your oppressors
> will come and bow down to you;
> all who reviled you
> will fall facedown at your feet.

They will call you the City of the Lord,
Zion of the Holy One of Israel.
Instead of your being deserted and hated,
with no one passing through,
I will make you an object of eternal pride,
a joy from age to age. ...
> Violence will never again be heard of in your land;
> devastation and destruction will be gone from your borders.
> You will call your walls Salvation and your city gates Praise.

Daniel 9:24 [emphasis added]:
> Seventy weeks are decreed
> about your people and your holy city—

to bring the rebellion to an end,
to put a stop to sin,
to atone for iniquity,
to bring in everlasting righteousness,
to seal up vision and prophecy,
and to **anoint the most holy place**.

Joel 3:18[emphasis added]:
> **In that day** the mountains will drip with sweet wine,
> and the hills will flow with milk.
> All the streams of Judah will flow with water,
> and a **spring will issue from the Lord's house**, watering the Valley of Acacias.

Haggai 2:7-9 [emphasis added]:
> I will shake all the nations so that the treasures of all the nations will come, and I will fill **this house** with glory," says the Lord of Armies. "The silver and gold belong to me"—this is the declaration of the Lord of Armies. [9] "The **final glory of this house will be greater than the first,**" says the Lord of Armies. "I will provide peace in this place"—this is the declaration of the Lord of Armies.

Millennial Kingdom of God on Planet Earth

Zechariah 6:12-15 [emphasis added]:
You are to tell him: This is what the Lord of Armies says: Here is a man whose name is Branch; he will branch out from his place and build the **Lord's temple**.

Yes, he will build the **Lord's temple**; he will bear royal splendor and will sit on his throne and rule.

There will be a priest on his throne, and there will be peaceful counsel between the two of them. The crown will reside in the Lord's temple ... People who are far off will come and build the Lord's temple, and you will know that the Lord of Armies has sent me to you. This will happen when you fully obey the Lord your God.

Zechariah 8:3, 6-7, 20-23 [emphasis added]:
The Lord says this: "I will return to Zion and **live in Jerusalem.**

Then Jerusalem will be called the Faithful City; the mountain of the Lord of Armies will be called the **Holy Mountain.**" ...

"Though it may seem impossible to the **remnant** of this people in those days, should it also seem impossible to me?"—this is the declaration of the Lord of Armies. The Lord of Armies says this: "I will save my people from the land of the east and the land of the west. I will bring them back to live in

Jerusalem. They will be my people, and I will be their faithful and righteous God." ...

The Lord of Armies says this: "Peoples will yet come, the residents of many cities; the residents of one city will go to another, saying: Let's go at once to plead for the Lord's favor and to seek the Lord of Armies. I am also going. Many peoples and strong nations will come to seek the Lord of Armies in Jerusalem and to plead for the Lord's favor."

The Lord of Armies says this: "In those days, ten men from nations of every language will grab the robe of a Jewish man tightly, urging: Let us go with you, for we have heard that **God is with you**."

Through his prophet Haggai the LORD God Almighty predicted that...
The latter glory of this house (referring to the Millennial Temple) will be greater than the former, and in this place I shall give peace.

Since true peace was not associated with the rebuilt Temples under Zerubbabel or Herod, or the false peace associated with the Jewish Temple rebuilt during Daniel's Seventieth Week [the Tribulation], the Haggai prophecy has to refer to a future temple during the Millennium – [one described in great detail in Ezekiel chapters 40-48], because the WORD of God informs us that there will be no temple after the

Millennial Kingdom of God on Planet Earth

Millennium ends and the Eternal Kingdom of God, the Father begins:
> I did not see a temple in it, [post-Millennium Jerusalem], because the Lord God the Almighty and the Lamb are its temple. The city does not need the sun or the moon to shine on it, because the glory of God illuminates it, and its lamp is the Lamb. [WORD of GOD in Revelation 21:22-23] [272]

Ezekiel records God's promise of the Millennial temple in great detail including the return to the Millennial Temple of God's Shekinah glory which had departed from the temple of Solomon and has not been in any of the other temples since then. [273]

Millennial sacrifices are mentioned in Isaiah 56:6-7; 60:7; 66:18-23; Jeremiah 33:18 and Malachi 3:3-4.

Further, Zechariah 14:16-21 speaks of the observance of the Feast of Tabernacles in the Messianic Kingdom but that feast required special sacrifices as part of its observance.

---

[272] In his Defender's Bible comment on Haggai 2:9, Henry Morris opines that this can only be a reference to the future millennial temple, for it was never accomplished in the restoration temple or in any other since. Furthermore, in this future temple--and not before-Christ will finally "give peace" to the world.
[273] Ezekiel 40:1 - 47:1. As to Shekinah Glory: Ezekiel 10:18,11:23; then 43:1-9.

Therefore, more than one passage and more than one prophet would have to be allegorized away if there is no Millennial Temple or Millennial sacrifice.

As J. Dwight Pentecost says:
"The glorious vision of Ezekiel reveals that it is impossible to locate its fulfillment in any past temple or system which Israel has known, but it must await a future fulfillment after the second advent of Christ when the millennium is instituted.

The sacrificial system is not a reinstituted Judaism, but the establishment of a new order that has its purpose the remembrance of the work of Christ on which all salvation rests. The literal fulfillment of Ezekiel's prophecy will be the means of God's glorification and man's blessing in the millennium".[274]

---

[274] J. D. Pentecost, *Things to Come*, Zondervan, 1978, 531

Millennial Kingdom of God on Planet Earth

The Millennial Temple as described by Ezekiel:

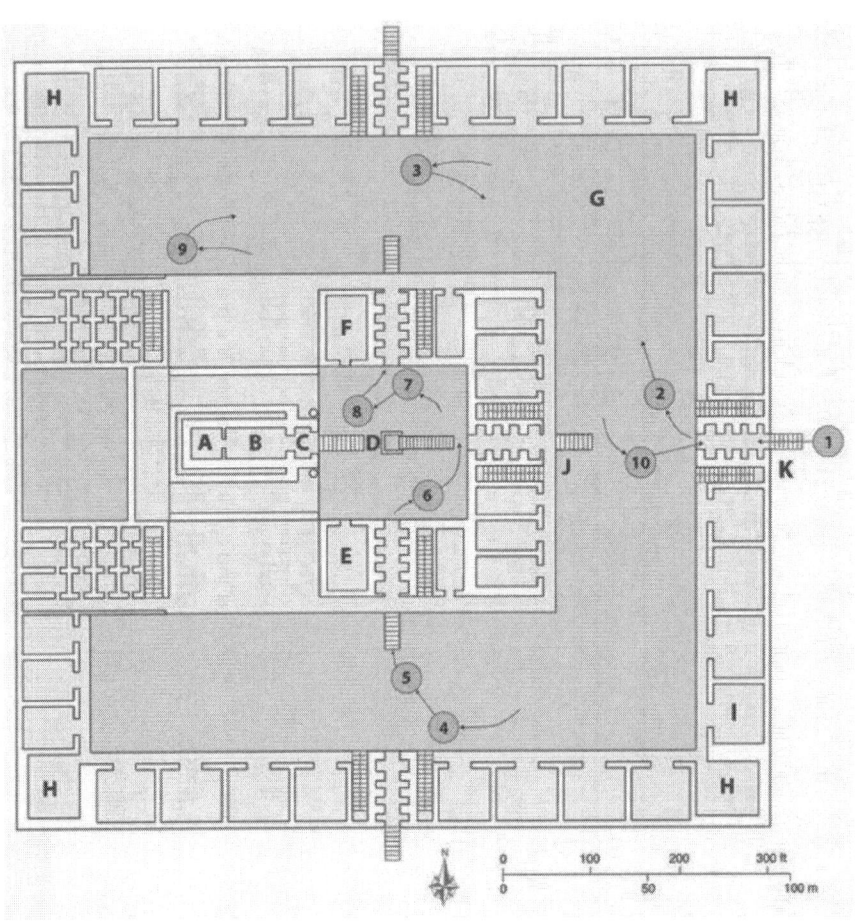

References:
A=Most Holy Place
B=inner room of the temple
C=entrance to temple

D=Altar
E=chamber for Zadokite priests
F=chamber for "priests who have charge of the temple"
G=outer court with 30 chambers in outer wall
H= temple kitchens
I=30 outer chambers
J= prince's gate
K= East gate, through which "the glory of
 the God of Israel" will return.

Ezekiel's Future Temple
Tour Explanation

#	
	References are to Biblical text in Ezekiel
1	40:6 Tour begins at eastern (main) gate. Note the East–West axis of the temple. A line drawn from the east gate to the Most Holy Place shows a sequence of three elevations as space in the inner temple becomes more constricted.
2	40:17 Ezekiel is shown main features of the "plaza" area from this vantage point.
3	40:20 Northern-facing gate.
4	40:24 Enroute to the southern-facing gate, area architectural details not provided.
5	40:28 Ezekiel's entry to the inner court is by way of its south gate
6	40:32 ... then to the east gate (past the altar)
7	40:35 ... on to the north gate, which includes areas for handling sacrificial animals.

Millennial Kingdom of God on Planet Earth

8   40:48 Ezekiel approaches inner temple structure itself describing its entrance;
        41:1 he remains outside the entrance while his guide measures interior/exterior.

9   42:1 They exit the inner court through north gate to explore the northwestern quadrant of the outer court.

10   42:15 Ezekiel and his guide leave the temple via the east gate. From this vantage point, Ezekiel was able to watch the return of "the glory of the God of Israel" moments later (Ezekiel 43:1-5).

The rebuilt Temple in Jerusalem will serve as a worship center for peoples of the world.[275]

Summary - The question of why there are animal/ blood sacrifices in the future Millennial Temple is a question over which numerous scholars have struggled to answer.

I believe there will be sacrifices but must admit that I am not absolutely certain as to why they will be required.

The previous discussion should give you food for thought if you too wrestle with this question. Below are a few of the resources which I have studied

---

[275] Isaiah 2:2-3, 56:6-8

that might give some assistance as you study this fascinating topic:

Arnold Fruchtenbaum -
  The Millennial Temple: Literal or
  Figurative? *Ariel Magazine*. spring-2016, p. 16-23

Jerry Hullinger -
  The Problem of Animal Sacrifices in Ezekiel
  40-48, *Bibliotheca Sacra*, July-September 1995

John Whitcomb - Christ's Atonement and Animal
  Sacrifices, *Israel Grace Theological Journal* 6.2 - 1985

Anthony Garland –
  Q 207 Sacrifices in the Millennial Kingdom
    Spiritandtruth.org

Thomas Ice - Literal Sacrifices in the Millennium
Thomas Ice - Why Sacrifices in the Millennium?
    The Pre-Trib Research Center (pre-trib.org)

John L. Mitchell,
  The Question of Millennial Sacrifices - Part 1
  Bibliotheca Sacra 110:439 1953. See also Part 2.

Gotquestions,org
    What is the significance of Ezekiel's temple?

A C Gaebelein - *The Prophet Ezekiel* (explanation
                                  of why sacrifices?)

Millennial Kingdom of God on Planet Earth

Chapter 14
Between the Millennium and the Eternal Kingdom

THE LAST REVOLT
SECOND WAR OF GOG-MAGOG

Scripture: And after the thousand years, Satan will be released from his prison, and he will come out to deceive the nations which are in the four corners of the earth, Gog and Magog, to gather them together to the war; the number of whom is as the sand of the sea. They went up over the width of the earth, and surrounded the camp of the saints, and the beloved city. Fire came down out of heaven from God, and devoured them. The devil who deceived them was thrown into the lake of fire and sulfur, where the beast and the false prophet are also. They will be tormented day and night forever and ever.

[WORD of GOD in Revelation 20:7-10]

THE FACTS:[276]

1. The Campaign of Armageddon will be followed by 1,000 years of peace as Jesus of Nazareth, the Messiah reigns from Jerusalem as King of King and Lord of

---

[276] Adapted from David R. Reagan, *What Are the Wars of the End Times? 7-9*, http://www.lamblion.us/

Millennial Kingdom of God on Planet Earth

Lords.

2. Satan will be bound for 1.000 years.

3. Everyone going into the Millennium in the flesh will all be saved people.
    But they will have children and begin to repopulate the earth. Their children will come to a point in their lives where they will decide to believe in Jesus or not.
    The point that the Bible makes is that some will not become believers.

4. Sin and crime will be greatly reduced. But, there will still be rebellion in the hearts of some who are born during that Millennium. Those living in the flesh will deeply resent the fact that they cannot freely pursue their worldly lust because they know that if they step out of line there will be instant punishment because justice will be swift, certain, and sure during the Millennium.

5. Accordingly, when Satan is released at the end of the 1,000-year Millennial period, some will unite in one last great rebellion against the LORD God Almighty in the tenth war of the End-Times [277]—— the Second Battle of Gog – Magog. These rebellious peoples of the world,

---

[277] For full information on the Ten Wars of the End-Times see Chapter 6 of Bob Chadwick, *Days of Destiny*.

led again by the then leader (Gog) of Magog, will join the released Satan in a revolt trying to overthrow Jesus.

6. This Second War of Gog-Magog will be the last war of human history.

7. Eternal peace is coming!
War is going to be gone forever. This hope of mankind will not be achieved by diplomats. It will be a gift of God through Jesus Christ, the Prince of Peace, who died to redeem mankind and all of the cosmos.[278]

Adversaries during the Second War of Gog-Magog: Satan, Gog (Leader of Magog) and rebellious Millennium-born humans versus Jesus, the Messiah.[279]

Motivation of Attackers:
Replace the Theocracy of Jesus, the Messiah.

Outcome: Fire will come down out of heaven from God and devour the rebels.[280]

Reflection: History is going to end as it began. It began with two people in a perfect environment who

---

[278] See Dr. David R. Reagan, *What Are the Wars of the End Times?* 7-9
[279] Revolution 20:8-9
[280] Revelation 20:10

rebelled against God. It is going to end up with all of humanity living in a perfect society, but some will make the same decision to rebel against God.

One of the many purposes of the Millennium, and perhaps one of the most important, is for God to prove to mankind that humans have an inherent sin nature that can only be redeemed by the Holy Spirit through faith in Jesus Christ.

The religion of Satan has always been Humanism — the belief in man. This philosophy teaches that Man is inherently good and capable of perfection through education and social justice. Humanists believe that if society can be perfected, mankind can be transformed and also be perfected.

In contrast, the Bible teaches that mankind is fatally flawed with a sin nature that makes people naturally evil.

The Bible teaches that the only solution to the sin problem is the transformation by the Holy Spirit that begins when the person accepts Jesus Christ as Lord and Savior.

God will prove this beyond a shadow of a doubt when He puts all of mankind into a perfect society for a thousand years and yet mankind still responds with rebellion.[281]

But, the Lord God Almighty will prevail against the rebels.
> Eternal peace is coming!
> War will then be gone forever.[282]
> And, also the LORD, sitting on a Great White Throne, will determine the fate of the unrighteous dead.

GREAT WHITE THRONE JUDGMENT

Scripture: I saw a great white throne, and him who sat on it, from whose face the earth and the heaven fled away. There was found no place for them. I saw the dead, the great and the small, standing before the throne, and they opened books. Another book was opened, which is the book of life. The dead were judged out of the things which were written in the books, according to their works. The sea gave up the dead who were in it. Death and Hades gave up the dead who were in them. They were judged, each one according to his works. Death and Hades were thrown into the lake of fire. This is the second death, the lake of fire. If anyone was not found written in the book of life, he was cast into the lake of fire. [WORD of GOD in Revelation 20:11-15]

---

[281] Adapted from Dr. David R. Reagan, *What Are the Wars of the End Times?* 7-9 http://www.lamblion.us/2015/06/what-are-wars-of-end-times-7-9.html
[282] See Revelation 21:4, 24-27

Millennial Kingdom of God on Planet Earth

THE FACTS:

1. Having not accepted the free gift of forgiveness and eternal life offered by Jesus of Nazareth, the Messiah, the non-believing dead will be judged according to their works while living on earth.

2. The Great White Throne will be the site of this final judgment.

Reflection:

The Great White Throne judgment, described in Revelation 20:11-15, takes place after the Millennium and the conclusion of Satan's Final Revolt.[283]

The non-believing dead will be resurrected.[284] Then, at the Great White Throne judgment, books will be opened that contain records of everyone's deeds while alive on planet Earth.[285] Since these non-believers have not accepted the free-gift of forgiveness and eternal life offered by Jesus of Nazareth, the Messiah, Jesus, to whom the Father has given all judgment,[286] will justly reward or punish each one according to the records of their deeds while they were alive on planet Earth.[287]

---

[283] Revelation 20:7-9
[284] Revelation 20:12-13
[285] Revelation 20:12
[286] John 5:22,27
[287] See Psalm 28:4, 62:12; Romans 2:6; Revelation 2:23, 18:6, 22:12

In addition, another book, the Book of Life, will be opened at this time.[288] The Book of Life determines whether a person will inherit eternal life with God or remain forever separated from the Kingdom of God.

And after the Great White Throne Judgment, Planet Earth will be Re-Formed.

RE-FORMATION OF PLANET EARTH
The Facts:
1. Satan's last revolt at the end of the Millennium will leave the earth polluted and devastated.[289]
2. Accordingly, following the conclusion of that Last Revolt, God will take the Redeemed [Faithful Followers of Jesus, the Messiah], off this earth and he will place us in a New Jerusalem which he is now preparing. [290]
3. He will then consume the earth with fire to burn away the pollution of Satan's last revolt.[291]
4. Out of the fiery inferno will come a New Heaven and a New Earth. Thus, the earth will be redeemed, refreshed Re-Formed and perfected.[292]
5. God will then lower the Redeemed down to this new

---

[288] Revelation 20:12
[289] See Revelation 20:7-9
[290] Dr. David R. Reagan, *Eternal Restoration or Fiery Finish?* retrieved from http://christinprophecy.org/articles/the-earth-in-prophecy/
[291] 2nd Peter 3:10-11
[292] Revelation 21:1

earth inside the New Jerusalem[293] and the Holy Trinity will return to earth to live in the presence of their Faithful Followers eternally.[294]

Reflection:

Satan's last revolt at the end of the Millennium will leave the earth polluted and devastated.[295] Thus, at the end of the Lord's Millennial reign, God will superheat this earth in a fiery inferno, burn off the dross and then refashion and re-form it. The result will be the "new heavens and new earth" prophesied in Isaiah chapter 66 and Revelation chapter 21.

This will be the perfected, eternal earth where the Redeemed [Faithful Followers of Jesus, the Messiah] will spend eternity in the New Jerusalem in the presence of God.[296]

READ ON ...

---

[293] Revelation 21:2, 10-23
[294] Revelation 21:3
[295] See Revelation 20:7-10
[296] Revelation 21:1-4

Chapter 15
Eternal Kingdom of God on Planet Earth

Tomorrow's World: the Permanent Presence of the Eternal Kingdom of the LORD God on Planet Earth

After God the Son's Messianic Millennial Kingdom and the re-formation of the Earth[297], the New Jerusalem descends to Earth and God, the Father joins God, the Son in the New Jerusalem on Planet Earth for eternity.[298]

The kingdom of heaven merges into the kingdom of God on Earth when Christ, having put all enemies under His feet, shall have delivered up the kingdom to God, the Father[299]

Scripture: Then I saw a new heaven and a new earth; for the first heaven and the first earth had passed away, and the sea was no more. I also saw the holy city, the New Jerusalem, coming down out of heaven from God, prepared like a bride adorned

---
[297] 2nd Peter 3:10
[298] Revelation 21:1-4, 22; Revelation 22:3-4
[299] 1st Corinthians 15:24-28

for her husband. I heard a loud voice out of heaven saying, "Look, God's dwelling is with humanity, and he will live with them. They will be his peoples, and God himself will be with them and will be their God.
[WORD of GOD in Revelation 21:1-3]

He then carried me away in the Spirit to a great, high mountain, and showed me the holy city, Jerusalem, coming down out of heaven from God... The twelve gates are twelve pearls; each individual gate was made of a single pearl. The main street of the city was pure gold, transparent as glass. **I did not see a temple in it, because the Lord God the Almighty and the Lamb are its temple.** The city does not need the sun or the moon to shine on it, because the glory of God illuminates it, and its lamp is the Lamb. The nations will walk by its light, and the kings of the earth will bring their glory into it. Its gates will never close by day because it will never be night there. They will bring the glory and honor of the nations into it. Nothing unclean will ever enter it, nor anyone who does what is detestable or false, but only those written in the Lamb's book of life.
[WORD of GOD in Revelation 21:10, 21-27 emphasis added]

Then he showed me the river of the water of life, clear as crystal, flowing from the throne of God and of the Lamb down the middle of the city's main street. The tree of life was on each side of the river, bearing twelve kinds of fruit, producing its fruit every month. The leaves of the tree are for healing the nations, and there will no longer be any curse. The throne of God and of the Lamb will be in the city, and his servants will worship him. They will see his face, and his name will be on their foreheads. Night will be no more; people will not need the light of a lamp or the light of the sun, because the Lord God will give them light, and they will reign forever and ever.

[WORD of GOD in Revelation 22:1-5]

The Biblical Facts:

1. Satan's last revolt at the end of the Millennium will leave the earth polluted and devastated.[300]
2. Accordingly, following the conclusion of that Last Revolt, God will take the Redeemed [Faithful Followers of Jesus, the Messiah], off this earth and he will place us in a New Jerusalem which he is now preparing. [301]
3. He will then consume the earth with fire to burn away the pollution of Satan's last revolt.[302]
3. Out of the fiery inferno will come a New Heaven and a New Earth. Thus the earth will be redeemed, refreshed and perfected.[303]

---

[300] See Revelation 20:7-9
[301] Dr. David R. Reagan, *Eternal Restoration or Fiery Finish?* retrieved from http://christinprophecy.org/articles/the-earth-in-prophecy/
[302] 2nd Peter 3:10-11
[303] Revelation 21:1

Millennial Kingdom of God on Planet Earth

4. God will then lower the Redeemed down to this new earth inside the New Jerusalem[304] and the Holy Trinity will come to earth to live in the presence of their Faithful Followers eternally.[305]

Reflection:
Satan's last revolt at the end of the Millennium will leave the earth polluted and devastated.[306] Thus, at the end of the Lord's Millennial reign, God will take the Redeemed off the earth, place them in the New Jerusalem[307], and then cleanse the earth with fire.[308] God will superheat this earth in a fiery inferno, burn off the dross and then refashion it. The result will be the "new heavens and new earth" prophesied in Isaiah chapter 66 and Revelation chapter 21.

This will be the perfected, eternal earth where the Redeemed [Faithful Followers of Jesus, the Messiah] will spend eternity in the New Jerusalem in the presence of God.[309] There will be nothing evil in the New Jerusalem for there will no longer exist anything that is cursed because sin and illness and death are gone.[310]

---

[304] Revelation 21:2, 10-23
[305] Revelation 21:3
[306] See Revelation 20:7-10
[307] Dr. David R. Reagan, *The Earth in Prophecy*, p.2, at http://christinprophecy.org/articles/the-earth-in-prophecy/
[308] See 2nd Peter 3:10-13
[309] Revelation 21:1-4
[310] See Revelation 21:27, 22:3; Dr. David Reagan, *The Earth in Prophecy*, **p. 2**

THE BLESSINGS OF THE ETERNAL KINGDOM
Biblical Facts:
- **New heaven and a new earth will have been created.**[311]

- **the saints of the Highest One will receive the kingdom and possess the kingdom forever, for all ages to come.... the time has arrived when the saints take possession of the kingdom**[312]

- **The holy city, New Jerusalem, will descend, coming down out of heaven, from God.**[313]

- **The LORD God Almighty will dwell there with Jesus and his people**[314]

- **The sea will be no more.**[315]

- **God will wipe away all tears from peoples' eyes**[316]

- **No more death**[317]

---

[311] Revelation 21:1
[312] Daniel 7:18, 22
[313] Revelation 21:2
[314] Revelation 21:3 "No more sea" does not necessarily mean "no more water." It simply indicates that the new earth will have a different arrangement as far as water is concerned.
[315] Revelation 21:1.
[316] Revelation 21:4
[317] Revelation 21:4

Millennial Kingdom of God on Planet Earth

- **No more mourning** [318]

- **No more crying** [319]

- **No more pain** [320]

- **There will no longer be any curse** [321]

- **There will be nothing evil in the New Jerusalem for there will no longer exist anything that is cursed [because sin and illness and death are gone].** [322]

- **People will see God's face** [323]

- **God will welcome the Overcomers**[324] **and be their God.**[325]

- **New Jerusalem will contain both the Throne of God, the Father, and Jesus, the Messiah.**[326]

---

[318] Revelation 21:4
[319] Revelation 21:4
[320] Revelation 21:4
[321] Revelation 22:3
[322] See Revelation 21:27, 22:3; Dr. David R. Reagan, *The Earth in Prophecy*, p.2.
[323] Revelation 22:4
[324] See John 16:33; Romans 12:21; 1st John 2:13-14, 4:4, 5:4-5; Revelation 2:7, 11, 17, 26; 3:5, 12, 21; 5:5; 17:14; 21:7
[325] Revelation 21:7
[326] Revelation 22:3

- **A River of Water of Life will proceed out of the throne of God, the Father, and Jesus.**[327]

- **The Tree of Life will be in the New Jerusalem; its leaves are for the healing of the nations.**[328]

- **New Jerusalem will be 1,500 miles long, 1,500 miles wide and 1,500 miles high.**[329]

- **New Jerusalem's walls will be 216 feet high.**[330]

- **New Jerusalem's wall will have 12 foundations, each bearing name of an Apostle.**[331]

- **New Jerusalem will have 12 gates each one bearing the name of a Tribes of Israel.**[332]

- **God's name will be on our foreheads.**[333]

- **New Jerusalem will not have a sun or moon.**[334]

- **There will no longer be any night in the New Jerusalem; they will not have need of the light**

---

[327] Revelation 22:1
[328] Revelation 22:2
[329] Revelation 21:16 [New American Standard Bible]
[330] Revelation 21:17
[331] Revelation 21:14
[332] Revelation 21:12
[333] *Ibid.*
[334] Isaiah 60:19; Revelation 21:22

of a lamp nor the light of the sun, because the Glory of God and Jesus will provide illumination.[335]

- New Jerusalem will not have a temple for God the Father, and Jesus, God the Son, are its temple.[336]

- And, the reign of God: the Father and the Son, will last forever and ever![337]

It is the New Jerusalem descending from heaven as the eternal home of God's people that compels the prayer of the saints at the conclusion of book of Revelation:
>
> **Maranatha**
> **[which means in English]**
> **"Amen. Yes, come, Lord Jesus"**[338]

Will you not join with us in this paradise?

Read on …

---

[335] Revelation 21:23; 22:5
[336] Revelation 21:22
[337] Revelation 22:5
[338] Revelation 22:20

Chapter 16
Passport to Enter the Kingdom

HOW DOES ONE BECOME A CITIZEN OF THE KINGDOM?

Although his grace makes citizenship available to anyone who will receive it, Jesus warned that it would be very difficult to enter his Millennial Kingdom and few would do so.

Scripture
- Jesus replied, "I assure you: Unless someone is born again, he cannot see the kingdom of God.". [WORD of GOD in John 3:3]

- I assure you," He *[Jesus]* said, "unless you are converted and become like children, you will never enter the kingdom of [God].
  [WORD of GOD in Matthew 18:3]
  [comment: Unless you dramatically change your way of thinking and become teachable, with the wide-eyed wonder of a child, you will never be able to enter into the Kingdom]
  Jesus answered, "I assure you: Unless someone is born of water and the Spirit, he cannot enter the kingdom of God. Whatever is born of the flesh is flesh, and whatever is born of the Spirit is spirit.

Millennial Kingdom of God on Planet Earth

[equivalent to being born again; water could symbolize physical birth, but more likely symbolizes spiritual cleansing which brings renewal; see Ezekiel 36:25–27],

- Do not be amazed that I told you that you must be born again. [WORD of GOD in John 3:5-7]

- Enter through the narrow gate. For the gate is wide and the road is broad
 that leads to destruction, and there are many who go through it.
 How narrow is the gate and difficult the road that leads to life, and few find it.
    [WORD of GOD in Matthew 7:13-14]

- The works of the flesh are obvious: sexual immorality, moral impurity, promiscuity, idolatry, sorcery, hatreds, strife, jealousy, outbursts of anger, selfish ambitions, dissensions, factions, envy, drunkenness, carousing, and anything similar.
 I tell you about these things in advance—as I told you before—that those who practice such things will not inherit the kingdom of God.
    [WORD of GOD in Galatians 5:19-21]

Who will become Citizens under Jesus's rule?
Over whom will He rule?

At the time of Jesus' birth, "wise men from the east" came seeking the "King of the Jews".[339]

Pontius Pilate likewise asked Jesus if He were the "King of the Jews," and Jesus affirmed that he was.[340]

But will Christ's authority be limited to the tribes of Judah and Benjamin—commonly called "Jews" today—when He returns?

The Bible shows that the coming Kingdom will encompass more than just the Jews—more than even all of Israel.

The coming King will be given "*the nations* for [His] inheritance, and *the ends of the earth* for [His] possession".[341]

Psalm 22 also prophesies: "*All the ends of the world* shall remember and turn to the LORD, and *all the families of the nations* shall worship before [Him]. For the kingdom is the LORD's, and He rules over *the nations*".[342]

Jesus revealed this truth to Nicodemus. When Nicodemus came to Him at night, Jesus told him,

---

[339] Matthew 2:1-2
[340] Matthew 27:11; Mark 15:2; Luke 23:3; John 18:33, 37
[341] Psalm 2:8
[342] Psalm 22:27-28 [emphasis added]

Millennial Kingdom of God on Planet Earth

"Most assuredly, I say to you, unless one is *born again*, he cannot see the kingdom of God".[343]

Paul told the Corinthians "flesh and blood [mortal humans] *cannot* inherit the kingdom of God; nor does corruption inherit incorruption".[344]

While we have a physical, flesh-and-blood body, we may be *heirs* of the Kingdom, but we cannot enter fully into the Kingdom, nor can we see it, until we become spirit—given a glorious spirit-composed body in the resurrection. This means that, even though all of mankind will be *subject* to the Kingdom that Christ will rule on earth, they will not necessarily be citizens of it.

The apostle Paul makes it clear in his letter to the Corinthians that physical flesh and blood cannot *inherit*, or fully enter into, the Kingdom of God.[345]

However, through the *resurrection* of those begotten by the Holy Spirit of God during this physical life, the mortal life then *puts on* immortality, and we become immortal, incorruptible, and enter fully into the very God Family—the Kingdom of God. It is only our spiritual *birth* that takes place when we receive God's Spirit. Our glorification—analogous to full spiritual

---

[343] John 3:3
[344] 1st Corinthians 15:50
[345] 1st Corinthians 15:50-54

maturity—does not take place until after we are resurrected.[346]

Just as the resurrection from the dead will not take place until the Second Coming of Jesus, the Messiah,[347] Christ returns), so inheriting the Kingdom will not happen until *after* He returns and judges the peoples of the earth at the Judgment of the Sheep and the Goats.[348]

The Millennial Kingdom of God will then be ruled by Jesus Christ and will be inherited by those who have been glorified upon being resurrected from the dead. The resurrected saints—citizens of God's Kingdom—will rule along with Jesus Christ over the remaining peoples of the earth.[349]

---

[346] Adapted from *Who Are the Kingdom's Subjects and Citizens?*, retrieved at https:www.truegospel.org /index.cfm/fuseaction/basics.tour/ID/5/.htm
[347] 1st Corinthians 15:51-52. See also Matthew 24:31; 1st Thessalonians 4:16-17
[348] Matthew 25:31-34
[349] Daniel 7:27; 2nd Timothy 2:12; Revelation 2:26-28; 5:9-10; 20:4-6; 22:5

[Source: https://hopeforourtimes.com/come-to-jesus/](https://hopeforourtimes.com/come-to-jesus/)

How Do You Become Born Again?

1. *Realize* that you have fallen short of Will of God. No matter how good a life we try to live, we still fall miserably short of being a good person. That is because we are all under the power of sin. The Bible says, "No one does what is good—not even one." We cannot become who we are supposed to be without

Jesus Christ.[350]

2. Recognize that Jesus Christ died on the cross for me and you.
The Bible tells us that "God showed His great love for us by sending Christ to die for us while were still sinners."[351]

This is the Good News, that God loves us so much that He sent His only Son to die in our place when we least deserved it.

3. Repent of your sin.
The Bible tells us, "Repent of your sins and turn to God, so that your sins may be wiped away."[352] The word repent means to change our direction in life. Instead of running from God, we can run toward Him.

4. Receive Jesus Christ into your life.
Becoming a Christian is not merely believing some creed or going to church. It is having Christ Himself take residence in your life and heart. Jesus said, "Look, I stand at the door and knock. If you hear my voice and open the door, I will come in . . ."[353]

---

[350] Romans 3:9-12 [New Living Translation]
[351] Romans 5:8 [New Living Translation]
[352] Acts 3:19 [New Living Translation]
[353] Revelation 3:20

Millennial Kingdom of God on Planet Earth

If you would like to have such a relationship with Christ, simply pray this prayer and mean it in your heart.

**"Lord Jesus, I know I am under the power of sin. .
I believe You died for my sins.
Right now, I turn from my sins and open the door of my heart and life and permit for me to enter your eternal Kingdom.
I confess You as my personal Lord and Savior.
Thank You for saving me. Amen."**

And the WORD of the LORD God Almighty tells us:
> **The message is near you, in your mouth and in your heart.
> This is the message of faith that we proclaim:
> If you confess with your mouth,
> "Jesus is Lord,"
> and believe in your heart that God raised him from the dead, you will be saved.
> One believes with the heart, resulting in righteousness, and one confesses with the mouth, resulting in salvation.**[354]

---

[354] Romans 10:8-10

Chapter 17
The Final Chorus

YOUR ETERNAL FUTURE IS IN YOUR GRASP

And so my reader, thus will begin your eternal destination of being a king and a priest before our God, to lead other men and women who enter the Millennium to the saving knowledge of Jesus Christ.

We will rule righteously and give the message of the Gospel of Jesus Christ unto the living mortals who still have their free moral will to accept or reject the message.

We will not coerce anyone to believe and accept, but as Jesus does by His Holy Spirit now, we will point them to the same cross that we came to know, and the same perfect sacrifice that we accepted upon our own lives for the remission of sins, our Lord, Savior and soon coming King, Jesus Christ.

So come Lord Jesus, yes, Amen. Come my Lord. We await our reward of being kings and priest before You. That is our glorious future of all who believe on His name, by faith and obedience to His call.

Millennial Kingdom of God on Planet Earth

Will you be counted as being changed into the likeness of Almighty God? Or will your future be different, because you have rejected His call, rejected His payment for your sins in His own blood.

Today, not tomorrow, is the time to make your future sure and set in stone. In comes down to the object of the whole writing of Holy Writ, your Bible, in this one passage in your Bible, the point of the whole Bible:

> **For God so loved the world, that He gave His only Begotten Son, that whosoever believeth in Him, shall not perish, but have everlasting life.**[355]

> **For God did not send his Son into the world to condemn the world, but to save the world through him.**
> **Anyone who believes in him is not condemned, but anyone who does not believe is already condemned, because he has not believed in the name of the one and only Son of God.**[356]

It is that simple...believe on the Lord Jesus Christ, as the Son of God, who was crucified for your sins and mine, raised from the dead, and lives forevermore, waiting to return to Earth, and so we shall ever be with the Lord.

---

[355] John 3:16
[356] John 3:17-18

Accept Him by faith into your heart and soul, with a simple prayer of repentance for being a sinner and needing a Savior for all have sinned and come short of the glory of God.

Then turn from worldly, sinful ways and follow the Savior of the world. That Savior, is Jesus my Lord.

Oh, won't you join us, those who have already accepted Jesus as personal Savior? It will be most glorious, and unimaginable to contemplate what God has in store for us who believe on Him by faith.

1. The WORD of the Lord God Almighty instructs and assures us that our immortal souls live forever despite the fact that our physical bodies (Earth-suits that we wear) age and ultimately fail.
[WORD of God: John 3:16; 3:36]

2. We have been granted the privilege to determine where we will live in Eternity by accepting or rejecting God's offer to become a citizen in his Eternal Kingdom of God.
However our choice:
    a. is limited to either spending Eternity with God in his Eternal Kingdom or outside that Kingdom eternally separated from God; and
    b. that choice must be made before our earthly body dies. [WORD of God: Matthew 7:13-14, 21-23]

Millennial Kingdom of God on Planet Earth

3. To help us decide our Eternal Destiny, the 66 books of The WORD of the Lord God Almighty provide us with a detailed description of the conditions that will prevail when his Kingdom returns to Planet Earth.

4. The choice is yours.
Choose this day whom you will serve throughout eternity.
And as you decide, do not rely solely on my research (or anyone else's), but rather be more fair-minded like the Bereans by examining The WORD of the Lord God Almighty daily to see if these things actually true.
[WORD of God: Acts 17:11]

What you believe about Bible prophecy has no effect on where you are going to spend eternity; it is not related to your justification.

But it has an immediate impact upon your sanctification, upon how you walk before the Lord in this life.[357]

Come Lord Jesus!
Our Blessed Hope

Maranatha !

---

[357] Dr. David R. Reagan, *Are we really in the Millennium now?*, p. 8

Millennial Kingdom of God on Planet Earth

Days of Destiny

The Tribulation and the Final Seven Years of Human Rule on Planet Earth

Compiled by Bob Chadwick

Compiler Bob Chadwick is a 91-year old retired United States Marine Corps Brigadier General and lawyer who believes everyone should know what the Hebraic/Christian Scriptures tell us about the future so they are prepared and can check the veracity of the biblical text against history and occurring events.

Available at Amazon.com.

Appendix I.
Begun in Genesis brought to completion in Revelation

Human history began in Eden, a Garden of Paridise and ends in a New Jerusalem, a city, like a garden paradise that will be the eternal home for God's Faithful Followers.

The WORD of God states in Revelation 21:5-7:
   the one seated on the throne said,

   "Look, **I am making everything new**."
   He also said, "Write, because these words
   are faithful and true." Then he said to me,
   "**It is done!** I am the Alpha and the Omega,
   the beginning and the end. I will freely give
   to the thirsty from the spring of the water of
   life. The one who conquers will inherit these
   things, and I will be his God, and he will be
   my son.   [emphasis added]

Millennial Kingdom of God on Planet Earth

What was begun in Genesis is brought to completion in Revelation, as the following listing demonstrates:

Genesis	**Revelation**
Heavens and earth created [Gen.1:1]	New heavens and earth [Rev. 21:1]
Sun created [1:16]	No need of the sun [21:23]
Night established [1:5]	No night there [22:5]
The seas created [1:10]	No more seas [21:1]
The curse announced [3:14-17]	No more curse [22:3]
Death enters history [3:19]	No more death [21:4]
Man driven from the tree [3:24]	Man restored to paradise [22:14]
Sorrow and pain begin [3:17]	No more tears or pain [21:4]

Appendix II. – End-TIMES Library

Booklet	Title
\multicolumn{2}{GuideBooks in Preparation from Amazon.com [listed under author Bob Chadwick], or Wisdom Press, Box 4888, Carmel, CA 93921 $8.95 each + $2.00 postage E-mail: EndTimesLibrary@outlook.com as to availability}
00	The Overcomer's Facts of Life
01	God Exists
02	Life Instruction Manual: 66 Vols.
02A	Master Plan of History
03	MYSTERY-Who Removed the Divine NAME of the LORD God Almighty from the Bible?
04	The Truth-Teller – the Messiah-King
05	The Inward Power – the Holy Spirit
06	Spiritual Communication: Prayer

Millennial Kingdom of God on Planet Earth

07	Two Roads-Two Destinations
08	Covenants of Lord God Almighty
09	Prophetic Signs of the Times
10	Understanding Israel's Unique Relationship with the LORD — Replacement Theology
11	Ten Wars of the End Times
	THE GATHERING STORM
12	Ascendant Powers Seek Global Primacy - One-World Government
13	Rise of Commercial Babylon - One-World Economy
14	Rise of One-World Religion - Religious Babylon
15	Agents of the Apocalypse: False Prophet Revealed – Powerful Religious Figure Leads a Religious Revival
16	Rapture of Bible-Believing Followers of Jesus

17	**Agents of the Apocalypse: Anti-Christ Revealed Charismatic World Leader Arises**
18	**Covenant of Pseudo-Peace with Israel**
19	**LORD God Almighty and Jerusalem**
20	**New Third Temple Construction in Jerusalem**
20 A	**Kingdom of Heaven Parables – inter-advent Period**
21	**THE DAY of the LORD GOD ALMIGHTY BEGINS Tribulation period of seven-years**
	First Quarter of Tribulation Period (21 months)
	THE SEAL JUDGMENTS
22A	**The Four Horsemen of the Apocalypse**
22	**Horseman #1 (white)-Peaceful Earthly Conquest and Dominion**

Millennial Kingdom of God on Planet Earth

23	Horseman #2 (red)- War and Persecution
24	Horseman #3 (black)- Famine-disease-injustice
25	Horseman #4 (pale green)- Death/Hades
26	Great Earthquake (6th Seal)
27	144,000 Israeli Evangelists
	Second Quarter of Tribulation Period (21 additional months)
28A	**THE TRUMPETJUDGMENTS**
28	Trumpet 1 – Hail, Fire and Blood
29	Trumpet 2– Mountain burning with fire
30	Trumpet 3- Falling Star: Wormwood
31	Trumpet 4- Sun, Moon and Stars Darkened
32	Trumpet 5 - 1st Woe: Locusts of Apollyon Plague men
33	Trumpet 6 – 2nd Woe: 200 million Horsemen Kill 1/3 Mankind

	Mid-Tribulation **3½ Years into Tribulation** **Period**
34	Peace Covenant with Israel Broken
35	Abomination of Desolation in the Temple in Israel
36	Tribulation Solar Flares
37	666 – Mark of the Anti-Christ
38	Two Prophets from LORD God Almighty Return of Elijah Prophets Killed, Resurrected, Translated Great earthquake same hour as resurrection of two prophets
	Last 3½ Years of Tribulation Period
39A	**THE BOWL JUDGMENTS**
39	Bowl 1- Malignant Sores upon Anti-Christ worshippers
40	Bowl 2 - Sea Turned To Blood
41	Bowl 3- Rivers/Springs Turned to Blood

Millennial Kingdom of God on Planet Earth

42	Bowl 4 - Sky-Scorching Heat–sun burning men with fire
43	Bowl 5 - Darkness and Torment
44	Bowl 6 - River Euphrates Dries Up
45	Bowl 7 - Great Earthquake & Hail
46	Fall of One-World Religion - Religious Babylon
47	Fall of Commercial Babylon
48	Siege of Jerusalem
49	Armageddon Campaign Gathering at Armageddon Campaign Battles of Armageddon
50	The Second Coming- Heavenly Signs the Second Coming of the LORD
51	75-Day Interval Between Second Coming & Millennium
52	Messianic Millennial Kingdom of God, the Son
53	The Final Revolt–Gog of Magog II.
54A	FUTURE OF MIDEAST NATIONS
54	Southern Jordan – Edom
55	Central Jordan - Moab

56	**Northern Jordan - Ammon**
57	**Saudi Arabia – Ishmaelites (one of fathers of all Arabs)**
58	**Egypt – Hagarenes**
59	**Lebanon – Gebal**
60	**Lebanon – Tyre**
61	**Sinai Peninsula – Amalek**
62	**Gaza Strip – Philistines**
63	**Iraq and Parts of Syria – Assyria**
64	**Syria – Damascus**
65	**Iran – Elam - Persia**
66	**ISIS/ISL: Clash of Civilizations**
67	**Apocalyptic Islam - End-Times Predictions**
68	**America Under Attack**
69	**Great White Throne Judgment - Resurrections**
70	**Eternal Kingdom of God**
71	**Overcomer's Pathway to Eternal Life - God's Rescue Plan**
72	**CHART - Countdown to Eternity**
73	**Ark of the Covenant**

Millennial Kingdom of God on Planet Earth

74A	Daniel's Prophecy of 70 Weeks
74B	Prophecies of Daniel
75	Jesus Foretells the Future (Olivet Discourse)
76	Glory of the LORD God Almighty
77	Satan
78	Heroes of the Faith – Hebrews
79	The Tree of Life
80	Book of Revelation Reveals the Future of Mankind
81	Is National Israel the Mother-in-Law of the Christian Church?
82	The Watchman

Above GuideBooks available from
Amazon.com
[listed under author Bob Chadwick]
or
Wisdom Press, Box 4888, Carmel, CA 93921-4888
$8.95 each + $2.00 postage

[E-mail: EndTimesLibrary@outlook.com as to availability]

Appendix III.
ABOUT THE AUTHOR

Bob Chadwick, a 91-year old Evangelical Christian, is a Team Director of Pointman Leadership Institute. As such he has taught Trustworthy Inspirational Leadership and Methods to Combat Corruption to Governmental leaders on 24 missions in 16 nations throughout the world.

Prior to that, Bob served 30 years in the United States Marine Corps, retiring as a Brigadier General and thereafter, as a lawyer, worked in Silicon Valley during the onset of the computer age.

As a student of the Hebraic/Christian Holy Scripture Bob endeavors to communicate Biblical information in simple, understandable terms. He seeks to check the facts and then discover and convey the truth from the WORD of God, history and reality rather than just simply following

and echoing the traditions of mankind.

Bob has earned a Doctor of Jurisprudence (J.D.) degree from Columbia University School of Law and also holds a Bachelor of Arts (Phi Beta Kappa with Honors and Special Distinction) degree from Columbia College at Columbia University, a Bachelor of Laws (LL.B.-Stone Scholar) from Columbia University School of Law and a Master of Laws (LL.M.) degree from New York University.

Printed in Great Britain
by Amazon